FADS AND FALLACIES
IN PRESENT-DAY EDUCATION

FADS AND FALLACIES IN PRESENT-DAY EDUCATION

By

HEINRICH EWALD BUCHHOLZ

Essay Index Reprint Series

BOOKS FOR LIBRARIES PRESS
FREEPORT, NEW YORK

First Published 1931
Reprinted 1971

INTERNATIONAL STANDARD BOOK NUMBER:
0-8369-2272-7

LIBRARY OF CONGRESS CATALOG CARD NUMBER:
75-156621

PRINTED IN THE UNITED STATES OF AMERICA

CONTENTS

	PAGE
FOREWORD	ix
AND A REPLY	xiii

Chapter
- I. INTRODUCTION ... 1
- II. LEADERSHIP PIANISSIMO,
  THE TALE OF A PEANUT ... 11
- III. ICHABOD WANTS A PORTFOLIO,
  HENCE A DEPARTMENT OF EDUCATION ... 30
- IV. MORE MONEY FOR LESS EDUCATION,
  BUT AMERICA IS YOUNG AND RICH ... 58
- V. THE POOR ENRICHED CURRICULUM,
  A TRIUMPH FOR THE PROGRESSIVES ... 87
- VI. PRUSSIANIZED PEDAGOGUES,
  THE TEACHERS OF LIBERTY ... 119
- VII. PUBLIC EDUCATION FEMINIZED,
  FALLACY OF EQUAL SALARY SCALES ... 150
- VIII. SAMPLE SCHOOLBOOKS,
  A STUDY IN POLITE GRAFT ... 170
- INDEX ... 193

FOREWORD

During the past twenty years, Mr. Buchholz has rendered to educators and to education a series of services that should go far toward offsetting whatever unpleasantness may accrue to the educational fraternity from his nimble wit and his passion for plain speech. He is and has been a publisher of educational books and periodicals of the more technical sort. Two highly specialized journals, *Educational Administration and Supervision* and *The Journal of Educational Psychology,* the former in its seventeenth year of publication and the latter in its twenty-second, were supported by him without profit, and sometimes at a loss, during the period when the interest of the teaching profession in the scientific study of its problem was slowly developing. He has also published a large number of important monographs, many of which, because of their technical character, could have but a slow sale and in the aggregate a small sale. Young men and young women, starting on their professional careers with high hopes but slender purses, have found in him a generous and kindly—albeit an extremely candid—friend.

Especially notable have been Mr. Buchholz's contributions to the development of public education in his own State and city. For more than a decade, over the pen name, Ezekiel Cheever, he wrote a column for the Baltimore *Sunday Sun*. In terse and simple language he set forth the educational needs of the city and of the State as he saw these needs. He was frank, sometimes almost to the point of brutality. He would not hesitate unmercifully to chastise his best friends if they strayed from what he regarded as the straight and narrow path of professional rectitude and unswerving fidelity to the public weal. Students of education who have followed the developments of the past ten years in Baltimore and Maryland will agree that the gratifying conditions now prevailing were made possible in no small measure by the keen critical analysis to which Mr. Buchholz subjected every educational proposal and by the skill with which he set his conclusions before the public.

The present writer is naturally out of sympathy with much that Mr. Buchholz has said about education and educators in his earlier satirical writings and with much that he says in the present volume. Almost necessarily, I suppose, satire involves exaggeration. Hyperbole has been characterized as the boldest figure in rhetoric and our author is a past master in its use. The initiated will not be deceived by these heightened color effects, but the layman should be frankly warned that here and there the picture is a bit distorted.

Taken as a group, schoolmen and schoolwomen are

not a bad lot. There is a good deal of Babbittry in the profession, it is true, but no more than in most of our occupational groups, and far less than in some. And the business of public education, in so far as the profession of teaching controls it, is undeniably cleaner in its administration and more efficient in its operation than any other branch of the public service with the exception of the scientific services of the federal government. Compare, for example, the administration of American education with administration of American law!

The extracts from courses of study included in Chapter V ("The Poor Enriched Curriculum") are—some of them, at least—sufficiently absurd to carry with them their own condemnation; but it should be said in all justice that these courses of study are not limited to such absurdities. As a matter of fact, each provides a fairly generous core of serious and substantial school work; and while the present writer has long opposed the particular brand of educational theory which these and many other present-day curricula reflect, and which the extracts selected by Mr. Buchholz most clearly exemplify, he would caution the lay reader against the inference that contemporary education has gone so completely daft as Chapter V might suggest.

Our author has a vigorous complex against the National Education Association and the Department of Superintendence, and some of his remarks regarding them seem a trifle unkind, to put it mildly. These organizations, however, are extremely important. They exercise upon the course of educational development in this country a most pervasive influence—an influence that is probably unparalleled by any other group of forces. For this very reason their policies and their activities should be subjected always to the closest possible scrutiny. The organizations are strong and vigorous. They are growing lustily. Criticism will not hurt them and justified criticism should serve to keep them in a position where they can render the best service to the profession and to the cause of education. Whatever they may reflect of smugness and self-sufficiency; whatever policies of mere expediency they may adopt or indorse; whatever unworthy means their members may employ to advance their own individual or group interests: these are legitimate objects of the satirist's darts and arrows.

* * * *

In his breezy Reply to this Foreword, the author suggests that I have spoken somewhat disparagingly of a book that I like—which is quite true. I like many things—and people—that do not agree with me. His further mild insinuation that in this Foreword I have been saying what I do not mean, I must just as mildly disavow.

WILLIAM C. BAGLEY

AND A REPLY

For no sensible reason Americans have come to regard all propaganda as necessarily evil. Occasionally only is the propagandist a wicked fellow as, for example, the writer, when he prevailed upon Professor Bagley to adopt one of his own practices in order that practices of that type might be condemned.

This book was ready for press when an eleventh-hour editorial conference was called. The meeting was loaded against me; therefore, it was safe to insist that reference to schoolmasters as "pedagogues" might give offense, and that the revelation of certain follies of activity programs might give the impression that no good could come out of any activity program.

My faith in the intelligence of those who may read this book would not permit me to intersperse the text with suggestions that a little sugar be sprinkled here and that a statement there must be taken with a grain of salt. I proposed to the Editor, who, incidentally, for the past twenty years has been my pedagogical counselor, that he produce a preface which would provide all the sugar and salt necessary. Hence the Foreword.

Evil propaganda lies in the fact that Professor Bagley has been persuaded to censure a work which he likes. He has chuckled over portions of the text and he has even read sections of the proof to his classes. In short, there is much closer agreement between the Foreword and the text proper than may appear on the surface, and also, I suspect, between the Editor and the Author.

H. E. B.

FADS AND FALLACIES
IN PRESENT-DAY EDUCATION

FADS AND FALLACIES IN PRESENT-DAY EDUCATION

CHAPTER I

INTRODUCTION

I

A strange phenomenon of contemporary education is the seeming aversion of most pedagogues to criticism of their craft and its practitioners. Outstanding representatives of the profession are quick to join issue with those who presume to discuss critically and for lay consumption the things attempted or proposed by any one in education. As a consequence, when an educational charlatan is being pilloried deservingly or some pedagogical quackery needfully exposed, it is not uncommon to behold high-grade schoolmen taking up the cudgels in defense of a something which their professional souls must loathe.

This attitude might easily be misinterpreted as the outcome of a fine sense of guild loyalty, calling for admiration despite its illogic. But, honestly, it springs from no such virtuous source. The pedagogue of quality dislikes having his weaker brethren and their projects openly censured, primarily because he fears that if education of any type is discredited before the layman, then all educators, including himself, may find it difficult to hold public confidence. Since he lacks faith in the common sense of the masses—a thing about which at times he prates like a soap-box orator—he is dead set against having them sit in judgment upon the goings-on in his craft. Hence selfishly he shields and defends notorious quacks, thus opening the way for these imposters not only to waste the people's money, but to trifle with the schooling of the people's children.

This state of affairs is lamentable. It accounts for such conditions as are gently condemned in the pages that follow; erects serious obstacles in the path of real educational progress; and tends to misguide laymen who should be thoroughly enlightened concerning public education. If representative educators were willing to be aggressively critical always, they would not necessarily thereby hazard the public's good will—their willingness itself would be sufficient to correct many of the ills that these educators now dread having revealed to the people. Once let the mountebank in education understand that substantial schoolmen stand ready to expose him publicly the moment he starts any foolishness with the schools, and he will be quick to seek other fields in which to practice his wiles.

II

Under existing conditions it is natural to anticipate a condemnation of the present volume by certain well-meaning pedagogues. Whatever the alleged grounds for protest, the concealed reason in most instances will be the protestant's fear of having aught in education condemned. Illuminating in this connection have been such comments as were called forth by the publication of certain portions of the book in magazine form. For example, the paper on the circumscription of the teacher was pronounced a gross misrepresentation by a number of normally honest schoolmen—it revealed in an undignified light a most dignified profession. One teacher, having damned the article unconditionally as false, promptly added that its publication left her in a quandary—should she terminate an acquaintanceship of many years' standing with the writer or invite the displeasure of her superiors and friends in the profession by being seen with him? In short, the sweet creature denied that such a situation as is pictured actually exists; then, naïvely, admitted that its existence curtailed her freedom in the matter of choosing her associates.

The article on school costs called forth much censure. Typical is a rejoinder which Superintendent Isaac O. Winslow contributed to his home-town paper, the *Providence Journal*. Taking exception to the statement that quantitativeness has been made the measure of educational progress, Mr. Winslow would like to know[1]—

If the American people are inclined to beautify their cities and towns by some expense for architectural attractiveness in their school buildings, who is so narrow and void of artistic taste as to regard this disposition as a fault rather than as a virtue?

Of course, Mr. Winslow did not meet the point at issue. The amount of money appropriated for a building—quantitativeness—will not determine whether that structure is to be beautiful or even efficient. A school building costing half a million may be much more artistic than one costing three millions. Indeed, too often costly buildings are made hideous with excessive ornament.

III

In my early journalistic days I came in contact with a printer who was assigned to the make-up editor. He was a snip of a human being not more than five feet tall and could easily have been carted about in a market-basket. A dozen times I have heard this man rave about some wonderful creature he had just seen on the street. Always it was the same story: "Oh, but today I saw a most beautiful woman—she was more than six feet tall and weighed all of two hundred pounds!" To him feminine beauty was massiveness.

[1] Providence (R. I.) *Journal*, March 17, 1929.

Complexion, features, proportions, grace meant nothing; but a whale of a female was his conception of perfection.

Many small contemporary pedagogues reveal a like mind-set when it comes to judging a school building. The area it covers, the weight it placed upon the backs of the taxpayers—these are accepted as the criteria for determining whether or not the structure is beautiful. They have no standard for judging real architectural grace, nor could they conceive of so elusive a thing as spiritual beauty. To illustrate this latter quality: a certain city decided to erect a new building for one of its high schools. Taking account of the actual needs in the case, an adequate and creditable structure could have been erected at an expenditure of one million dollars. However, the proposal was made to lay out more than three times this sum. A few conservatives opposed the proposal, not only because such an expenditure would represent willful extravagance, but in the same city many elementary classes were being conducted in shacks called portables. An expert was called in and overruled the objections of the conservatives. Subsequently, in a small intimate group, this expert was asked whether he regarded the costly structure as justified, taking account of the pressing needs of other school children. He admitted frankly that his personal judgment had been against the elaborate building, but he said that the alumni of the high school, an aggressive organization, were "hot" for a gigantic, showy building, and he thought it unwise to oppose them.

It is possible, of course, that he was not disturbed so much by the threatened hostility of the alumni as by a fear that if, in this single instance, he—an outstanding expert—questioned the propriety of making a large outlay for a schoolhouse, the public might accept his course as an invitation to scrutinize all other building appropriations. But there it stands—three and a half million dollars worth of land and stone and trimmings in a city where many young children are being taught in dingy, unhealthful rooms. In the eyes of a truly democratic people this massive structure could have no spiritual beauty—it would be beastly—but seen by the eyes of a Mr. Winslow, "Who is so narrow and void of artistic taste as to regard the outlay as a fault rather than a virtue"?

IV

Coached by the forward-lookers in education, even the Baltimore *Sun,* which for thirty years has been buying my stuff, much of it on education, felt called upon to rebuke me editorially for the article. The *Sun* allowed that I demonstrated the "more money," but did not prove "less education," and added:[1]

Doubtless modern education has its extravagances and vagaries. But it remains to be shown that the efforts to broaden its scope, to extend its influence, to improve its

[1] The *Sun* (Baltimore), February 21, 1929.

INTRODUCTION 7

facilities, to study its work, to substitute for ancient dogma more enlightened methods are not worth while, especially in a rich and young nation.

Perhaps the reader who is not ready to justify extravagances and vagaries on the ground that America is a rich and young nation may see in the articles some suggestions of the "less education." Even the *Sun* will doubtless find the evidence it demanded in the complementary chapter, "The Poor Enriched Curriculum." America should spend as much money on education as school administrators can justify, but whenever a school administrator attempts to discredit the critic who insists that each item in the budget be justified, it is safe to conclude that the critic has put his finger on an indefensible outlay.

Again, America is justified in discarding any practice in education after experimentation has shown that there is a better method; but when experiments become the substitutes for tested and proved procedures instead of a search for better practices, then a halt should be called. The tendency in certain school systems is to conduct the schools in such fashion that some of the pupils—usually the bright ones—will get such education as they would be able to pick up independently of schools and teachers, while a great many of the pupils get very little or nothing; these are the ones for whose schooling the greatest responsibility rests upon public education.

When "Ichabod Wants a Portfolio" first appeared, leading educational groups in the United States were still keen for the department and rumors had it that one of the many commissions appointed by President Hoover would recommend a Federal Department of Education with its secretary a member of the President's cabinet. Certain outstanding proponents of the department promised a reply to my paper. Later developments, however, indicate that an attempt may be made by them to get from under the project. Even should the proposal for a department be discarded, temporarily or permanently, the discussion warrants republication because of the revelations as to how our leading educational organizations function. Moreover, it should give warning to American schoolmen to be very cautious whenever they are invited to join forces with any federal appointee in the field of education.

V

To give point to the foregoing statement, I may record an incident which occurred since the first publication of the article. Under date of August 15, 1930, some one associated with the press bureau of the White House Conference on Child Health and Protection, sent out the following communication to the educational journals:

My dear Editor:
  The division of Public Relations of the White House

Conference on Child Health and Protection is very anxious to carry to President Hoover a full report of magazine interest in this subject when the Conference convenes for its final meeting, November 22, 1930.

We are desirous not to omit any magazine which has printed articles about or made any reference to the Conference. We have some records of this but they are far from complete. I am wondering, therefore, if you will help us so far as your magazine is concerned.

You can help in two ways—first by giving us a list of all issues that have so far contained mention of the Conference or that will contain mention of it, and second by sending us a clipping of the material or a copy of the issue. In this way we shall be able to prepare a good report and to support it by an interesting exhibit.

I am enclosing a stamped and addressed envelope for your convenience in replying.

With cordial good wishes and the earnest desire to see that every magazine editor who has contributed in any way to public interest in the Conference shall receive recognition from the leaders of the Conference, etc., etc.

About the same time a lot of press matter, for immediate release, was sent out. Could there be anything cheaper or more insulting to the intelligence of even an educational editor than this? Is one to understand it as an insidious effort to get press matter into school journals by informing them that their names will be included in a list to be presented to the occupant of the White House? Apparently the only reason for using this gaudy bait is to get a great mass of clippings with which to fool the President and the American people into believing that there is widespread interest in the activities that he has set on foot.

VI

It may be that the papers here assembled will not prove pleasant reading for the average educator. The writer feels called upon to disclaim any wish to irritate or offend those who are truly interested in the welfare of American school children. The primary purpose of the book is to stir, if possible, American educators to a realization not only of their responsibility to give a decent performance on their own account—a thing which doubtless even now many fully sense—but to recognize their personal obligation to make it increasingly more difficult for the weak, the foolish, and the designing to prey upon the public schools.

CHAPTER II

LEADERSHIP PIANISSIMO

THE TALE OF A PEANUT

I

Once upon a time a pedagogical peanut aspired to become a pumpkin—and realized his desire. The transformation required neither magic nor a resort to prayer, but was accomplished easily by following a path which ineffectual leadership had permitted earlier like aspirants to blaze across the field of modern education. The incidents here chronicled could just as readily have occurred in any one of a score of American institutions of higher learning; therefore no particular significance attaches to the fact that they happened at Pierce University.

Twenty years before the story opens Pierce had established a College of Education as an integral part of the University. The College engaged to produce certificated workers for every sort of job imaginable in a school system; and in summer its lecture halls were crowded with teachers in service, many of whom came thither to have low-grade scholarship hastily and cheaply retouched.

The College boasted numerous specialized departments, including one devoted to subject matter and method in nature study. The enrollment in this section increased rapidly and was especially large during the summer term, so that its staff had to be augmented from time to time. And then, one pleasant spring day, President John Smith Adams made a not uncommon blunder in college administration—when appointing an additional instructor, he picked what vulgarians would term "a lemon."

II

Horatio Bump was a ladylike person with projecting teeth, concave chest, and a cancerous ambition. All he asked of any college president was enough room on the faculty for his size 12½ feet—confident that with such a footing he would be able readily to lift himself by his bootstraps to the dizzy heights of fame. On being named to a modest instructorship, he promptly began to train for the lifting feat.

Somewhere he had read that Dewey stressed the importance in education of the child's interest. That was as far as he felt it necessary to accompany Dewey. He asked himself what, from the viewpoint of the nature-study department, might be represented as the thing in which children reveal greatest interest, and his answer was "pets." Here truly was inspiration.

Next the youthful pedagogue turned to Bunk—just

long enough to get a line on the Bunk knack for assembling data in support of proposed curriculum revision. The "endless chain of objectives" worked out by a University of Bunkum professor made a strong appeal to Mr. Bump; and he spent several weeks in constructing elaborate lists of objectives in all of the common-school subjects. Then with graphs he demonstrated graphically how each objective could be tied up securely with the child's inherent interest in bugs, worms, and other animals.

With the opening of the summer term, Mr. Bump was assigned several groups of school teachers who were willing to swelter through their vacation in hot lecture halls—with thought less of increasing their efficiency than their pay. When he entered his first class, he was confronted by a sorry collection of languid humanity. But he dispelled the languidness in the twinkling of an eye. Right off the bat he announced that his was to be no conventional course where students would be required to buy textbooks, make notes, and take examinations. His mission was to make a revelation; and those who sat at his feet during the delivery of his message would get full credit for just the sitting. Tired pedagogues sat up and nudged one another—here was a proper dish for a summer session!

Bump announced that he had formulated a brand-new system of education which would effect as great economies in time and effort for overworked and underpaid teachers as had been accomplished, say, for domestic wives through the development of electric dishwashers, ironing machines, and the neighborhood delicatessen shop. His plan was so simple, the amazing thing was that it had not been discovered long before, bearing in mind how many other great minds had been seeking a sound foundation for a system of modern education.

Bump's science of education, to be known henceforth and forever as *petology,* rested firmly upon the child's interest in living things. A rosy picture was painted for the students whom fate had decreed should first receive the revelation—all they had to do was to get the basic idea clearly into their clever heads and their future would be assured. Going forth as disciples of the new education, they would be in a position to demand from their respective school boards unlimited consideration when the time came for making up the daily programs and—what was equally important—the budgets.

III

It required no mental effort to listen to Bump's prattle during the weeks that he held forth, and so his courses went over strong. He assured his hearers the time was just ahead when the world would have to acknowledge that a fearful blunder had been made by that historic schoolmaster who barred the classroom to Mary's Little Lamb. How readily the dear woolly creature would have lent itself to a motivating of arithmetic, reading, spelling, geography, domestic science, and homemaking.

Bump devised novel ways for driving home his claims. He spent one delightful session catching flies so as to demonstrate how, under petology, these winged insects could be utilized in making elementary mathematics a lively subject even for very young children. He put on a hilarious lesson in geography when he spread a wall map on the classroom floor and turned loose two grasshoppers, taken captive on the college campus that morning. It was great fun for the immature adults in his class to observe the places these insects visited, noting them down on paper and indicating their relative geographical positions.

He convinced his merry students that his new scheme of education would be welcomed with open arms by school children, who would rush breathlessly to class each morning, wondering what kind of living thing would be waiting there to give spirit to the classroom work. Also, he intimated slyly, the coöperation of school patrons would be quickly enlisted through setting aside specific occasions when adult outsiders might bring to school their Pekingese dogs, Maltese cats, and Harz Mountain canaries, and show them off to the gratification of the owners and the delight of the children. However, later on, after petology had become firmly established, the demand would be that every school have its own collection of living things, housing a fine assortment of rabbits, cats, dogs, mice, turtles, butterflies, caterpillars, and cockroaches in a specially constructed pettorium.

Bump did not worry his hearers with details as to how teaching was to be made more effective, or effective at all, through injecting his so-called petology into the various school subjects—his followers had to accept on faith his assurance that he had discovered the only practical system of education and that the system would work out its own perfection through being put into operation. He spent most of his time telling of the wonders that were to be accomplished for pets, pupils, and pedagogues—the three R's traveling hand-in-hand with the three P's. During the summer session, with no one attempting to obstruct his way, he got his idea going at a lively pace, and the members of his several classes were unanimous in acknowledging that "a good time was had all 'round."

IV

The father of this new science of pedagogy did not hide his light under a bushel, but managed from the very start to get considerable publicity. He poured out the sort of bizarre stuff that newspapers eat up without editorial mastication, and usually succeeded in having his portrait appear with each news item concerning his teachings.

It is natural, therefore, to assume that President Adams and the rest of the faculty at Pierce were early forced to take cognizance of what was going on under their very noses. If they had been too busy with their own duties to follow Bump's activities during class hours, they could not escape the bold headlines which the press so frequently gave to accounts of his performance. Assuming that these men, or some of them, were fit to hold their jobs, it follows that before the summer session had progressed far they must have realized that this delirious pedagogue threatened to turn loose a group of irresponsible followers who would throw a monkey wrench into the machinery of an educational system whenever they got a chance; also, that to intelligent people on the outside the circus Bump was putting on reflected no credit upon the University.

But president and professors kept silent. This silence, say in the case of Doctor Adams, might be interpreted as evidence that he was too dense to sense the asininity of petology or else too lazy to exercise his prerogative and stop the show. However, Adams was really neither dense nor lazy. The worst that could be said about him was that he had accustomed himself to follow certain practices, developed by contemporary college officials, which are useful primarily in clearing the way for quacks to attain preëminence while potential leaders stand by inactive.

The significant aspect of this affair to the reader is

not what Mr. Bump actually did, but the conditions that made it possible for a person of his calibre to discharge any function in the field of higher education. Therefore, the searchlight may be turned from him to the environment in which he found an opportunity to develop his idea. The corner stone of this environment is the executive head of the University.

President Adams started his administrative career with promise of becoming a real factor in the intellectual progress of the community. He was a man of exceptional ability—a clear head, sound scholarship, agreeable personality, and a saving sense of humor. There was every reason—but one—why he should have made a creditable college executive. His one shortcoming was that he was overawed by the dignity of his position. Whenever need for action arose, the need for action had passed by the time he got through debating whether the course he had in mind would be sufficiently dignified for the head of a great institution.

Upon his induction into office, persuaded that everything in his administration must always be serene, with never the semblance of a rumpus among those connected with the University, he formed the habit of taking counsel constantly with his trustees—a lay board which knew how to manage neither a college nor a college president. This body promptly infected him with its outstanding ailment—a fear of doing aught which might win the disapprobation of faculty, students, press, or public. For instance, except a faculty member was suspected of laxness in morals or deficiency in bandstand patriotism, he must be handled with kid gloves. No matter how impossible he might be as a teacher, he was not to be dismissed; rather the aim should be to procure for him a more responsible position elsewhere by recommending him highly to sister institutions.

Adams had sense enough to know that Bump should not be handled with kid gloves. The only logical course was to grab him roughly by his coat collar and the seat of his trousers and drop him from a third-story window. Such conduct on the part of the President would have been impulsive, righteously so; but it was not safe according to Adams' view for a dignified college administrator to be impulsive. Instead, therefore, he studied the problem from every possible angle, and the ramifications into which his meditations led him wove a mesh from which even an eel could not have extricated itself.

V

A survey of these ramifications will afford partial explanation of why educational leadership is ineffectual today in the United States.

First of all, the "fool" public, which never gave Pierce University anything but trouble, always came in for profound consideration by the President. What if the so-called man in the street is ever ready to criticize, on the curb and in the letter columns of the press, the way in which institutions of higher learning are run! Not having the slightest knowledge of what a college is or should aim to be, his criticism, if not ignored, might safely be accepted as warrant for running counter to his views. But this man in the street loomed up big when Adams contemplated dealing summarily with Mr. Bump. The affair might degenerate into a public scandal, from which Bump in all likelihood would emerge a hero to the rabble, while the President would be pictured as a clown, not through any sense of justice, but because the man in the street can get so much sport out of envisaging a high dignitary in a sheepish rôle.

Of course, Adams did not realize that he was giving the blind prejudice of the rabble precedence over his own sound judgment in deciding how to handle an administrative matter. He noted that Bump was the sort of go-getter who would be quick to turn any blow at himself to advantage by bellowing from the housetop that he had been fouled; and an attempt by the executive to silence him, either with or without dismissal, might be represented as another incident in the eternal war between the progressives and the mossbacks of education. Therefore, rather than be accused, falsely, of seeking to muzzle adult members of the teaching staff, he missed his opportunity to maintain a safe balance between common sense and damned foolishness in education.

Next, he felt, there were the customers to be considered. Pierce University, engaged in producing teachers, was really a manufacturing plant, and no such enterprise could hope to run for long unless it was able to sell its product. At all costs Pierce must not hazard whatever respect it might have among the prospective employers of its graduates. Adams felt it necessary to move cautiously, lest he direct attention to certain facts which he felt might profitably be concealed—not only had petology been launched at Pierce, but the founder of petology had received his professional training in the institution. If publicity were given to this, what would happen to the institution's reputation for turning out safe and sane pedagogues?

Again, Doctor Adams was always considering how his acts would be regarded by his board of trustees—an odd mixture of human beings. For example, there was Marcus Goldback—a conventional "big business" man, loaded down with wealth, conceit, and stupidity. But this fellow was being humored, always in the hope that when his last will and testament was opened, it would provide for a liberal bequest to the University. In the early days of that summer session during which petology was launched, Goldback had complimented the President upon having discovered "that live-wire, Bump." Mrs. Goldback was simply crazy about the man's humanistic philosophy!

Another member was John Knox Flint, a dyed-in-the-wool fundamentalist whose outstanding worth as a trustee was his ability, whenever the exchequer was near a state of collapse, to beg some emergency funds from saint or sinner—or perhaps a combination of the two as in the case of the foundations. Flint had coaxed a senile plutocrat to endow a chair of logic as a memorial to his illiterate parents and had persuaded the widow of a libertine to found a professorship in law to help the community forget the shortcomings of her late spouse. But he was forever asserting that his big task as a trustee was to purge the faculty of pagans. If he should learn that Bump had been dismissed because his teachings were unsound scientifically, what chance would the President have of longer defending those whose teachings were, in the eyes of Flint, unsound morally — the biologist who persisted in ridiculing fundamentalism and the history teacher who spoke as if socialism could ever become a respectable form of government?

VI

But to Adams, worse than the "fool" public, the customers, and the board of trustees, were the noisy, nosey alumni. The word flashed before his eyes a disturbing likeness of one Louie Swartzheimer, who had been "put through college" when his father, a prosperous butcher, donated funds for the library building. Louie purposely became active as an alumnus so as to keep before his townspeople the fact that he was a real college graduate.

It was Louie who suggested to his father the romantic idea of putting out a new brand of frankfurters, labeled "Pierce's Choice," and with a picture of the University on the package. When one of the professors innocently asked if the thing had been approved by the college officials, Louie became indignant and demanded to know whether Pierce was to be run by the professors or the alumni. Thenceforth his purpose was to make the answer "alumni," and he was untiring in his efforts to win other alumni to his side. He was literally in command of one of the most outspoken elements in this group of trouble makers, and would not be slow to seize on Mr. Bump as a convenient means of annoying the administrative office.

John Smith Adams confessed—to himself—that he had made a serious blunder in appointing Bump; but what to do? Occasionally he forgot his piety and actually prayed that the young instructor might conveniently be run down by a reckless automobilist, always stipulating in his prayer that the driver must do a thorough job. Then, unexpectedly, a storm broke.

In the midst of the hiring season for Pierce graduates, a group of people who were anti-everything grabbed a bit of Bumpian twaddle as an excuse for a general attack on the University. Adams was called on to defend the institution, and gave an interview which, in print, defended not only Pierce University, but Mr. Bump as well. The instant the newspaper was on the street, the President realized his mistake. He hurried to his study and, behind locked doors, took inventory of himself. He had started his professional career with the makings of a real man, but the presidency had converted him into a coward. He intended to hold on to the presidency like grim death, but, at the same time—damn the job!

VII

Perhaps it is unreasonable to expect a college president, loaded down as he is with no end of administrative cares, to assume the burden of professional leadership. The task of setting a proper standard and keeping the profession free from quackery might more properly be placed on the shoulders of the professorial staff. But the faculty at Pierce, just as at many another similar institution, found all sorts of imaginary difficulties in the way when it seemed called upon to exercise assertive leadership. A cursory survey gives the impression that the first concern of each individual on the staff was to protect his own hide. By way of illustration, the case of a typical instructor, Lawrence Small, may be studied.

When the first report of Bump's ravings reached Professor Small, his impulse was to rush forth and do murder. The impulse was holy, but he promptly repressed it. He argued that he had a wife and two small children who by all means had to be spared the thrill of having the head of the household blazoned on the front page of the newspapers as another professorial murderer. Moreover, he was not at all sure that he would enjoy being hanged, even in so noble a cause as revenging an insult offered his craft. It was convenient for him to step off into the side lines, hoping that President Adams would ring down the curtain on the burlesque or that some fellow professor, as emotional as himself but without the encumbrance of a family, would do the necessary violence.

Later on, as things went from bad to worse and it seemed imperative for some one to take the initiative, Small permitted his pet brand of professional ethics to trifle with his conviction much as a cat plays with a captured mouse before devouring it. Repeatedly he sensed the need of protesting the show Bump was putting on, but always found some reason why *he* should not be the protestant. When far enough away from the University to run no danger of executing his plan impulsively, he jollied himself by pretending that he would give Doctor Adams the alternative of accepting his own resignation or demanding that of Bump; but in short order he would allow himself to be overwhelmed with fear that his bluff might be called, admitting that such a protest would really be a bluff, since, at his age of life, no other position would offer should his connection with Pierce be terminated.

The only honorable course, seemingly, was for some one to resign and then fire his broadsides not only at Bump, but also at Pierce for tolerating such a mountebank. However, Small felt that scant joy would come to him from such a course if, for the fun of firing, he had to expose to possible starvation the same wife and small children who previously had constrained him from committing murder. He even hesitated to speak frankly regarding the matter to his intimates on the faculty, lest he be suspected of disloyalty to the University. He had to remember that he, too, was but a teacher at Pierce, and had no business criticizing a fellow instructor.

Then, one morning, as he walked to the classroom where eleven students awaited him, he passed a lecture hall in which Bump was to hold forth. The place was filled to overflowing. His pride was crushed and his courage completely dissipated. This, he told himself, was what education had come to. If he opened his mouth now, the most apt response, a knockout, would be that he was envious of the new man's popularity. He decided to forget Bump; but the petologist would not be forgotten. That very noon the creator of petology burst rudely upon Small and a few associates who were lunching together at the faculty club with—

"I say, just as soon as you fellows get a chance, let's

work out a scheme for introducing petology into your courses."

That was the proper setting for rough stuff, but the members of Small's group smiled weakly and allowed the offender to strut off unmolested. In the same tragic week, President Adams was put on record in the newspapers with a defense of what was going on at Pierce, including the activities of one Horatio Bump. Then it was that Small consoled himself with the hope that the public schools would have courage enough to save not only themselves, but higher education as well, from the blight of Bumpism.

VIII

Bump had repeatedly demanded that his followers be recognized by school systems as experts in a new science of education. He was quick to capitalize the Adams interview. Here was evidence of what the "leaders" thought about petology. Not only did President Adams commend it, but no outstanding pedagogue anywhere had been able to find a single flaw in it, otherwise he would have been quick to expose it. Open the school gates and let the Bumpians in!

The last line of defense proved as weak as the first and second, and Bumpism invaded the schools. It got its first entrance in a system whose superintendent was himself a product of Pierce. In short order the Jones' Angora and the Brown's Chow chased out conventional reading, writing, and arithmetic. Naturally, the youngsters preferred a session with a real cat or dog to fretting over multiplication tables which could neither wag their tails nor lap up milk.

In the system, low-brow teachers—pioneers in the new education who had received their inspiration directly from the prophet Bump—began to pose as superexperts. At this, staid old pedagogues were tempted to send up a mighty howl of protest. But they, too, had been fed upon a brand of professional ethics which did not develop courage. Their whispered complaints reached the ears of the superintendent at the same time that a group of idle women, hot for a new fad, were commending him upon having admitted this humanizing influence into the city's educational system. Here at last was something for which even the antivivisectionists could stand!

The superintendent had to choose between these patrons, who, for all he knew, might hold his fate in the hollow of their hands, and teachers who, under his administrative discipline, were meek and long-suffering. In the uneven contest the teachers came out a poor second. By accepting what he, although a product of Pierce, suspected was not sound educationally, the superintendent put himself in a compromising position. But what schoolman would not prefer that to the danger of finding himself in no position at all? He closed his desk and the incident, and devoted the rest of his day to the improvement of his golf game.

As time passes, right down the line those who should have combated and destroyed Bumpism will be prepared, should need arise, to defend it rather than expose their past delinquency. Then petology will be in a fair way to establish itself as the panacea that is to cure all the ills bred by earlier systems of education. Textbooks in every subject based on the new science will pour from the press and into the classroom. Children will come to like school better—because it will interfere less with the frolics staged during class hours. Doctor Horatio Bump will loom forth as a mighty figure in American education, for which he will give praise to his own creative genius, rather than to an educational leadership which has grown spineless and afraid.

CHAPTER III

ICHABOD WANTS A PORTFOLIO

HENCE A DEPARTMENT OF EDUCATION

I

In the spring of 1918, when Mars sat atop the world and every American Tom, Dick, and Harry who could escape the draft began to dream of war-time profits, public education in the United States found itself in a precarious situation. Part of the teaching force had been recruited for military service; a larger part had deserted the classroom for highly remunerative employment in commerce and industry; and those teachers who stuck to their lasts were enduring privation for the loyalty.

It was at this time that a Commission on the Emergency in Education worked out the scheme for relief which found expression in the Smith-Towner Educational Bill. The outstanding feature of the proposal was an annual Federal appropriation of one hundred million dollars in aid of public education. For the distribution of this money, a department of education was

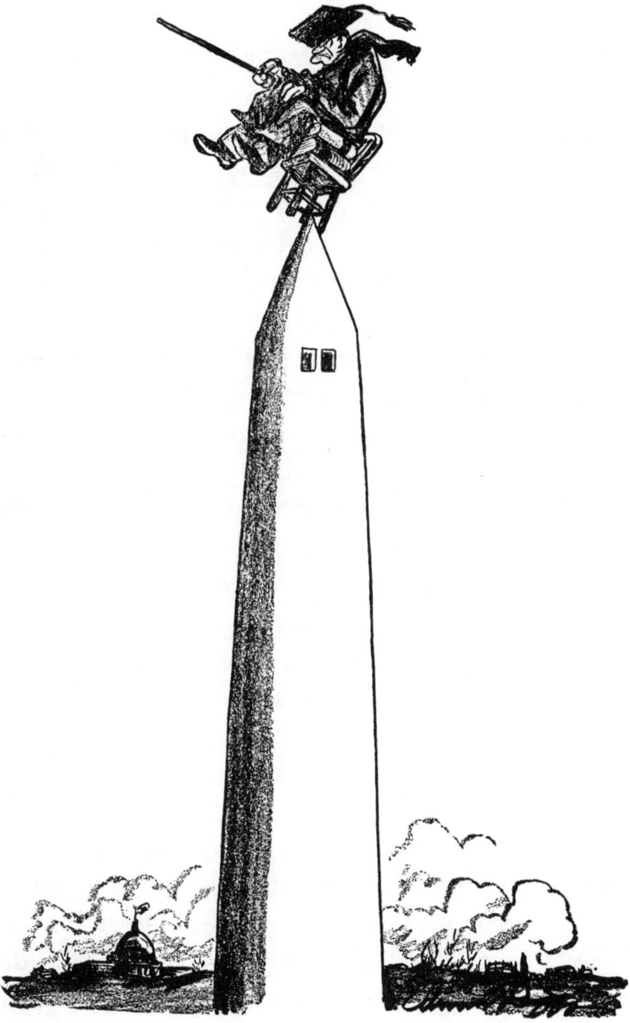

to be created with its chief executive holding membership in the President's cabinet.

Perhaps because, at the time, the proposal seemed both modest and honest, it did not arouse enthusiasm in a war-mad Congress, and the measure never reached a vote. In due course, the emergency in education passed. Most school systems, upon the return of Harding's normalcy, found ways for working out their own salvation. Nevertheless, since 1918 persistent campaigning and resolutioning have been carried on in support of various measures that have been presented in succession to the Smith-Towner Bill.

It would be unwise to insist that the schools now need such financial assistance as appeared imperative in 1918; therefore, this feature has been dropped. In the later forms of the proposal, educational research, originally accorded scant attention, is pictured as the urgent need of the country. The demand for a portfolio continues, since, it is alleged, a cabinet position is essential to create national educational leadership and give it fitting prestige.

Advocacy of the department has now become so much a habit with various educational groups, that an attempt to stop it would about parallel in its futility the endeavor of a proverbial old woman to sweep back the sea. The writer seeks no injunction against those educators who campaign for a Federal department and a portfolio of their own. But the average teacher who does not aspire to the secretaryship deserves a bit of consideration. He has been misled into believing that wonders will be accomplished for his craft through the creation of the department. It is a gracious thing for this average schoolman to get into line, especially at convention time, and, when the ringmasters crack the whip, to shout for a department. But since Congress ignores his shouting year after year, he should be able to find consolation in the speculation that he—and the country—may be better off without the department.

II

The business of the present discussion is to survey the proposal critically for the benefit of the average educator. An excellent starting point is provided by the utterance of two members of Congress who officially sponsored the latest rehashing of the measure. Representative Daniel A. Reed, of New York, speaking in the House on December 11, 1929, said[1]:

There are parts of this country, abundantly endowed with natural resources, where the lack of educational advantages has pauperized what should have been a land of plenty. Generations of boys and girls have had their mental and spiritual lives starved and stunted. The real loss to the nation, therefore, is not alone one of material wealth. The real tragedy is the useless sacrifice of a social and spiritual force, the potential possibilities of which the nation has no

[1] *Congressional Record*, Seventy-First Congress, Second Session.

moral or political right to stunt and repress, and one which it can ill afford to lose.

If Congress had had the vision to establish a department of education when it was first suggested by patriotic and far-seeing men and women, educational opportunities would have been, ere this, more nearly equalized and much of the neglected and unutilized latent power would have been made available to the several States and to the country at large. Tragic and suicidal as our policy may have been in the past in this respect, to neglect now to establish a clearing house of educational data, as we enter upon the greatest period of world-wide competition in trade and commerce in history, would be even more short-sighted and deplorable.

The bill which I have introduced provides, among other things, for research in the ever-expanding field of education. Why? Because research in the educational field is just as important, if not more so, than it is in the domain of business, agriculture, and industry. The discovery of a fact that will prepare a boy or a girl for success, measured in terms of usefulness to society, is more important by far than the discovery of a fact that will improve livestock, and I do not wish to minimize or belittle the importance of the latter.

It is quite as important to the taxpayer to receive accurate information with reference to heat, light, ventilation, sanitation, architectual designs, materials, and equipment for a school as it is to obtain reliable facts with reference to the construction of a cow stable or a hen house . . .

Education is not free when the latest educational data to which the Government has access is not obtained and made available to every teacher and every school board throughout the United States. There can be no equality of educational opportunity unless the Federal Government meets this responsibility, which it can and should meet . . .

Senator Arthur Capper, of Kansas, "went on the air" January 28, 1930, with a demand that America "Put Education in the President's Cabinet." The title alone might prompt the reader to conclude that Mr. Capper on that occasion discussed adult education for politicians. The following excerpts will prevent any such erroneous conclusions[1]:

I want to talk to you for a little while on our public schools. They are the gateway to good citizenship. They rank high among our most cherished American institutions.

Now I will ask you: Are you ashamed of our public schools? The question is not far-fetched. A visitor, unacquainted with our scheme of government, might well ask the same question. And why should he ask it?

Because every other important part of America's life is represented by a place in the President's cabinet. The national defense, the Federal courts, commerce in all its varied forms, labor, agriculture, and so forth, all have a department of their own in the Federal Government . . .

I have introduced in the Senate a bill to create a department of public education. The head of this department would be a member of the President's cabinet. The department's principal function would be to furnish reliable and

[1] By special permission this speech was printed in the *Congressional Record,* op. cit.

accurate information on educational programs and advanced methods of instruction to schools throughout the country . . .

Our children—all of them, regardless of race, creed, or station in life—are surely entitled to the Federal Government's attention and assistance in education. This would be particularly helpful to rural boys and girls. City children would also be helped.

We should have had this department of public education long ago. It is time that the great cause of education received fitting recognition from the people it has served so well. Every taxpayer in this land will be benefited through the various efficiencies and economies to be made possible by coördinating activities, elimination of duplication, and the giving of expert advice on schoolhouse construction, business management of schools, and the like . . .

I am confident that when all the people know the facts about this bill Congress will meet the public demand, enact it into law, and give to the people the benefits they are now denied.

Both of these learned statesmen have produced fine sentimental stuff for consumption by the electorate. However, when their statements, and those of others who favor the proposal, are scrutinized dispassionately, they do not carry conviction that a department of education with a portfolio for its secretary is essential; or that it could justify its existence by the data collected; or, finally, that as a consequence of any information which may be distributed, education in America will become more efficient or more economical.

III

It is well to differentiate between mere information and research. To obtain news of what most school systems, at home and abroad, are doing, is not difficult. Whenever an educational unit attempts something different, those responsible for the innovation rush into print with reports of the undertaking—and their own portraits. News of this kind, unless it can be critically analyzed by each separate schoolman, or else for him by some one competent and willing to determine the worth of the project, is not necessarily valuable to the cause of education.

A somewhat similar situation obtains in the matter of research—a word which today covers a multitude of educational sins. It requires a well-informed and scientifically trained person to select problems for research, to plan the work, to supervise its execution, and to appraise the findings. True, there is ample room for research in education, provided it is directed by those acquainted with earlier studies by others, and who have a proper technique, a clear conception of the purposes for which the schools exist, and courage. But, having allowed so much, it does not follow that a Federal department would constitute a promising agency for instigating or supervising such research.

There is a question—a serious question—whether any department of the Federal Government would attack educational research in a courageous, far-sighted, and critical spirit. The official tenant of the White House will always regard himself as responsible for what is done by the various Federal departments. That tenant would insist that neither the proposed department nor its secretary publish aught which might be construed as criticism of what any school might be doing. The proposed department could, of course, report what various schools were attempting, but if it shaped the statement in such wise that it appeared to condemn the venture, no matter how much condemnation might be merited, the President, other cabinet members, and every last congressman would jump on the neck of the secretary and his staff.

By way of illustration: At present there is an Office of Education (until recently known as a Bureau) in the Department of the Interior. This Office attempts in a modest way what a department of education would undertake on a larger scale. The Office has its experts who are neither better nor worse than the experts who, in greater number, would be put on the payroll of the proposed department. Its activities are directed by the same type of administrative officer as would get the portfolio—an executive appointed by the President.

Not so long since, this Office undertook a study of certain phases of elementary education. Hidden away in the report[1] of this study appears the following statement:

[1] Mary Dabney Davis. "Some Phases of Nursery Kindergarten-Primary Education, 1926-1928." *Bureau of Education Bulletin* 29, 1929. Washington: Government Printing Office.

The number of nursery schools listed by the Bureau of Education in 1926 was 67, and in 1928 it was 121. Many of the schools listed in 1926 did not continue and many new ones have since opened.

To a person who does not sense the need for a Federal employee to be severely noncommittal always, what single problem for study stands out on reading these lines? Why was it that "many of the schools listed in 1926 did not continue"? All else is of little consequence until the lessons to be found in the failures have been learned. But no attaché of the Office, nor of the proposed department, would trespass on such ground for fear that he might stir up officials in systems where nursery schools persisted and also certain lay bodies that engage on a national scale in propaganda for kindergarten and nursery schools.

IV

It would be polite, perhaps, to presume that the cautiousness which makes the efforts of the Office negative has annoyed American pedagogues and is responsible for the demand for a secretary of education with larger authority, so that the restraint may be removed. To forestall any such naïve conclusion, another illustration is offered. This reveals the influence that can be exerted upon the most powerful educational organization in America—the National Education Association (which, incidentally, is the chief sponsor of the proposed department)—the moment it feels it is functioning as an agency of the Federal Government.

Disturbed over an apparent breakdown in law enforcement, with special reference to prohibition, the President appointed a commission to make a critical survey of the situation. From time to time stories had appeared in the daily press indicating that transporting liquor to school in violation of the Volstead Act was not uncommon among public high school pupils. An honest and thorough inquiry into this matter would have much merit; a fake study, if accepted by State and public in good faith, would be an iniquitous thing, since it would conceal facts which should be brought into the open and faced courageously. The National Education Association, through its secretary, volunteered to investigate this phase of the big national problem for the President's Commission. Shortly after starting its investigation, the Association burst into print, February 17, 1930, with a report in part as follows:

> At the request of President Hoover's Commission on Law Observance and Enforcement the National Education Association arranged to coöperate with its plan to get facts which would show behavior conditions in the high schools of the country comparing 1930 with 1920. It will be some time before this work will be completed but enough reports have come in to show that conditions in the high schools are much better than in 1920 with respect both to drinking and to general behavior.

This statement, handed first to the press on the eve of an important national educational convention, was republished in the official organ of the Association and later issued as a poster. The poster was put on sale at a nominal price for quantity orders in the hope that various school systems would be enabled to spread the "glad tidings" among their students.

But pause and look into the merits of the investigation. If officials of the Association are qualified to conduct such an inquiry as they volunteered to make for the Federal Government, they should have known in advance that the data they undertook to gather would be unreliable and misleading. Questionnaires soliciting opinions—not facts—regarding drinking and behavior among high school pupils in 1930 as compared with 1920 were sent to principals of public high schools. The average high school principal is far removed from the social activities of the student body—he comes in contact with students, as a rule, only when called upon to act as a disciplinary agent in matters where teachers feel they are unable to cope with the situation. His guess, for instance, that the students' conduct in and out of school is satisfactory may be due to the fact that his teachers are handling their own problems of discipline or that the pupils have become so clever at breaking regulations as to escape detection. Again, the average high school principal would not dare go on record with an admission that conditions in his school were bad, for fear that such a statement might be interpreted by his superiors as a confession of his inability to handle his problems.

But the most significant flaw in the case is this: The questionnaires were sent to high school principals, asking them to make a comparative report on conditions in their respective schools in 1920 and 1930, whereas not 10 per cent of the 1930 principals had filled similar positions in 1920. In other words, fully 90 per cent of those to whom the forms were sent were not qualified to express even an opinion on the matter at issue. What is the import of this? It shows how little reliance can be placed on a research study, even though undertaken by leading groups of American teachers, when they presume that they are acting under the auspices of the Federal administration and should, in that rôle, produce the kind of *evidence* that will reflect credit upon the Government.

However, the thing does not stop here. The Association next seeks to inveigle innocent teachers over whom it holds sway into following suit. Witness the following item from the official organ of the Association[1]:

The statement by Secretary Crabtree on The Eighteenth Amendment and the Public Schools suggests a line of effort which every teacher can pursue for himself by comparing conditions now with conditions in saloon days. Many teachers will wish to give this statement to the editors of

[1] *Journal of the National Education Association*, April, 1930.

local and country papers. The new standards are here. They are here to stay and teachers can help the situation by creating a fuller understanding of the great gains that have been made in America under the new policy.

The same professional organization, which is the most ardent advocate of the proposed department of education, first works out a questionable report on existing conditions in a field with which it should be peculiarly well-informed, and then attempts to induce teachers to follow in its footsteps by creating and spreading unreliable opinions as facts. If the same spirit which actuates the Association the moment it regards itself as operating under Federal auspices could be given larger play, say, through a Federal department with unlimited funds and a cabinet officer for its head, the chief result doubtless would be steadily to make it more difficult for schoolmen and laymen to ascertain and publish the truth regarding public education.

V

Research in education is desirable only provided needed studies are undertaken and carried on by those qualified, mentally and morally, to do a decent job. There are numerous school systems now engaged in doing research on their own account. The officials of these systems are afforded opportunity, in various groups to which they have access, for reporting and discussing their findings. Suppose these research people should be called together by a secretary of education and started on their work coöperatively with that Federal official—at the very outset a handicap would appear in the demand that they defer to this secretary since he, no matter what his calibre, would stand forth as their professional superior. This secretary, because of his position in the Federal administration, would forever be guarding against the possibility of the group doing something that might offend any school system or the Administration. He would guard against this so carefully that he would soon have the group dizzy from moving around in a circle.

The American people will do well not to take literally the prattle by the sponsors of the educational bill about the present perilous position of the nation due to the failure up to now of the government to provide for educational research on a big scale. Such talk might easily give the erroneous impression that all schoolmen are hungry for reports on research, and that any shortcomings in contemporary public education can be traced directly to the nation's neglect in not having erected a huge research plant.

Research in education is being carried on in this country on a far vaster scale than in any other country and reports are made available promptly in state papers, periodicals, monographs, and books. Some of this material is free for the asking; some is sold. The amazing thing, in the face of this situation, is the indifference of so many schoolmen to this possible source of help.

This coldness is not due to the fact that some of the material is not free, since officials are able to purchase such material with public funds. That they do not procure and read is due to their apathy. No provision can be made by the proposed department for changing these schoolmen so that the instant a secretary of education opens the floodgates of research, the teachers will rush into the shower. Certainly their interest will not be stimulated by the assurance that, because of political expediency, all material produced by the Federal plant will be toned down to innocuousness.

Should the department, once it is established, find that educators are not taking its product in such manner as to warrant a further expenditure of the stipulated annual appropriation, or should the problems calling for research become exhausted, will the secretary dismiss his research experts, return all unused funds to the treasury, and ask that the department be abolished? To date the advocates of the educational bill have not given a promise on this score, and so the reader is free to speculate what course would likely be taken in such a situation by some future secretary of education. Mention of this leads to a consideration of the sort of individual who would probably grace the office of secretary.

VI

The demand for a secretary of education has been stressed from the very beginning of the agitation for a department. A portfolio, it is claimed, is the only means through which public education can be given dignified national leadership. It is possible to believe that American education may need a different type of leadership, and at the same time to doubt whether a desirable standard can be created through presidential appointment. There are two sides to the question: the kind of man who is likely to be appointed and the effect such appointment will have upon him.

The advocates of the department ask the American people to believe that only an outstanding educator would ever be appointed. For the sake of argument assume that the President will look about the country to find a man preëminently qualified to assume the rôle of commander-in-chief of America's educational forces. The next question is, would that man, if tendered the portfolio, accept it?

Try to picture a man with the essential qualifications —not a pussyfooter or professional climber or wire-puller; but a scholar, a critic and, to boot, a courageous man. Perhaps there are a few men in America who will fit the specifications—men who would bring prestige to the office. Any such man, being offered the portfolio, would naturally consider what the position might demand of him. He might ignore the professional sacrifice involved in stepping for four years or more out of his pedagogical environment and into the routine of a Federal post; but he would hardly be so dense as to overlook the sacrifice he might have to make of self-respect and dignity in order to fit himself into the traditional grooves of political life.

Would he be able to sit through dull sessions of the cabinet at which every question coming before the group had to be surveyed always from the standpoint of how the decision might affect the Administration's grip upon the electorate? Would he be agreeable to having congressmen fill his days with appointments to meet school groups whose representatives in Congress undertook to show them the Washington Monument, the Smithsonian Institution, and the Secretary of Education? Would he have the stomach to concern himself with such state problems as to whether Mrs. Longworth or Mrs. Gann should be given precedence at a social function? Would he be intrigued by a job which, because of its relation to political administration, imposed all sorts of restraint upon him even to the point where he would not be privileged to express his personal view on an educational question if that view was at variance with the position the President pleased to take on the same professional matter?

A big enough man for such a position as the proponents of the department picture the secretaryship, would decline the office for the very simple reasons, first, that it would cramp his style and, secondly, that his acceptance would remove from active participation in education a leader of the type that is sorely needed and unfortunately rare.

Having decided that the sort of man who could bring proper authority to the secretaryship would not accept the position if it were offered him, it is in order to look at the matter from another angle and see what chance there is that the office would ever be tendered to him. The champions of the bill ask the public to believe that, should a department of education be created, every future president will be so keen to preserve the inviolability of American public education that he will not consider anyone for the position except a very superior educator.

To accept this assurance, it is necessary to assume that a mere politician who can make the presidency may be counted upon always to display more interest in providing education with creditable leadership than is evinced by educators themselves. As American schoolmen today function in their professional organizations, the cheapest sort of politics and the most puerile form of sentimentality are permitted to be the determining factors in the selection of those who are to fill the highest offices. This charge applies to the female element no less than to the male. One of the women elected to the presidency of the National Education Association admitted subsequently that teachers who held subordinate positions under her had been transported to the place of meeting and provided with membership, at the expense of her campaign managers, so that the meeting might be loaded in her favor.

In late years, both in the Association and in its aristocratic offspring, the Department of Superintendence, aspirants for office have staged sordid campaigns of the kind that characterize ward politics. Through manipulations by the ringmasters, mediocre pedagogues have been dragged out of obscurity and pushed into offices that made them "national leaders." Ambitious individuals have carried on campaigns year after year for those offices which should have been conferred unsolicited only upon educators of outstanding professional attainments. Not so long since at a meeting of one of these organizations, a pedagogue who aspired to an office of secondary importance opened headquarters at a leading hotel in the convention city, engaged a large suite of rooms, and kept open house morning, noon, and night. He was assisted as host by a group of henchmen who received visitors, provided for those who cared to be refreshed, and electioneered brazenly for the hospitable campaigner. The man was elected.

VII

When leadership of the type now fostered by these organizations begins to function, the results are not edifying. At a convention to which more than ten thousand school people had come from all parts of the country, at public expense, to have their professional outlook broadened, the chief position on a main program was given to a woman politician who was layman to the craft; whose address was not above the high-school level; and who sought to make political capital out of her appearance. At another meeting, where an audience had been assembled presumably to hear educational leaders discuss vital problems, the session was devoted largely to nonessentials. Right of way was given to a government official who delivered an address in which he made a studied effort to express no definite views on anything lest his words be regarded as an official commitment. A group of old codgers was trotted on to the stage to have jingling medals pinned on. A couple of women qualified for membership in a mutual admiration society. By the time the buffoonery was over, the audience was too weary to follow anything but the inclination to get out of the hall.

So that there may be no charge of sex discrimination in the matter of distributing high offices, the National Education Association established the rule of rotating men and women in the presidency. A woman president, in whose hands was placed responsibility for shaping the entire program for an annual convention, made a brief contribution to the official organ of the Association from which the following interesting excerpt is quoted:[1]

Ignorance and narcotics tend to standardize, weaken, and defeat people. Education fosters individuality, distinction, and achievement. Has there been in all history so colossal

[1] E. Ruth Pyrtle in *The Journal of the National Education Association*, April, 1930.

a standardizing process—such a vast demonstration of the sheep-like qualities of the human race as in the spread of the tobacco habit?

Can we afford to spread, even among our children, a habit whose cost is greater than the total cost of free public education; a habit surely unworthy an age that has produced a Lindbergh . . .

This reference to the so-called Lone Eagle is introduced somewhat reluctantly, since Mr. Lindbergh should be pitied rather than scorned for the reckless enthusiasm of his worshipers. But the item is significant in revealing the type of appeal that leading educational groups today listen to and often indorse. In the first place, the factual data are inaccurate and misleading. In the second place, the implied proposal is so manifestly impracticable as to make the mention of it a sheer waste of printer's ink. The appeal is primarily to the emotions rather than to the judgment. And when Miss Pyrtle attempts to imply that the world owes the aviator any homage because he elects not to use tobacco, she apparently forgets that her hero, according to report, threatened to resort to the weed if the "Anti's" did not give up pointing to him as a model.

These revelations of what the foremost educational groups in the United States do when they are privileged to confer the standard of leadership and of the quality of the leaders they choose have a direct bearing upon a consideration of the proposed department.

There is no ground for presuming that a man elected President of the United States will set a better example when picking a secretary of education than is to be found in the precedents established by educators in electing officers for their professional groups. If a department should be created and run by the President without consulting the ringmasters of education, things might be bad; if these school politicians were consulted, they might be worse.

VIII

At all events, the office would likely go to a relatively small man. He would have unlimited funds available for hiring "research" workers to carry on at home and abroad. It is hardly necessary to picture the army of lame-duck educators that might be recruited, but it is important to consider the possibility that the office would be used at times against the best interests of education in the various States. The proposed department has been opposed as a threat against the sovereignty of the States in that it will give the Federal government control over courses of study and instruction. When such danger is mentioned, the champions of the proposal say "Bosh!" But the opportunities for a secretary of education to interfere in a hurtful way with the administration of state, city, and county schools cannot be dismissed in this way.

Regardless of how insignificant might be the man offered the portfolio in education, the moment he is confirmed as secretary he will stand forth in his craft as one who can speak with authority on every phase of education. This is no idle speculation. Evidence of it is found in the attitude which educators now assume toward the Commissioner of Education. The Commissioner, addressing ten or fifteen groups of specialists in various fields of education during a short convention, is accepted by each group as an expert in its special department. Of course, the utterances of a secretary of education would carry even more weight. Advocates of the department admit this when they point out the large influence for good a secretary of education might exert over school boards, civic bodies, and even legislatures. For *good?* Yes, on the assumption that the ideal man will get the office, and consequently for bad if the antithesis of the ideal is appointed.

Once more the leading educational organizations provide suggestive precedents. When a prominent schoolman retired from an important state superintendency in 1923, the ringmasters of these two organizations concentrated all the influence they could bring to bear in an effort to interfere with the governor in his endeavor to get a new superintendent. Each man considered for the position was promptly approached and urged to refuse the position as a rebuke to the governor for having allowed the former appointee to retire. To the educational organizations, as their feelings were reflected by the ringmasters, the good of the schools of the State was as nothing compared to the importance of avenging an alleged injustice to a schoolman.

When Henry S. West retired from the superintendency in Baltimore, the Department of Superintendence, through its secretary, burst into print with a protest which, no matter what its original purpose, seemed capable of being effective primarily in preventing Baltimore from getting a competent man for the vacancy. Sherwood D. Shankland, the secretary, wrote:

The fundamental factor producing the West resignation was the undoubted fact that Dr. West had made himself an obstacle in the way of City Hall's quiet but effective domination of the school system. Those in a position to know have no hesitation in declaring that no superintendent can succeed in Baltimore until the school system is relieved of political and financial domination by the Mayor and Board of Estimates. An independent Board of Education, with members elected at large by the people of Baltimore, must be established before any far-reaching program of educational progress will stand a reasonable chance of success.[1]

If, as implied, this announcement was based on information from those in a position to know the Baltimore situation, then they were guilty of willfully misrepresenting the case to Mr. Shankland. When he proclaimed that Baltimore's only hope lay in an elected school board he, innocently perhaps, lent the weight

[1] School and Society, June 20, 1925.

of his official position to the effort to put over on Baltimore a scheme that was favored by a few ringmasters in the Department, but which certainly did not have the endorsement of a majority of the members. Fortunately, Baltimore did not accept the prescription. Since that time, however, a far-reaching program of educational progress has been inaugurated. This assertion is based on public utterances even by those who doubtless earlier prompted Mr. Shankland to propose an elected board.

A secretary of education, bearing in mind the weight his words would have, could easily inject himself into any local situation either because he might naturally be meddlesome or else because politicians and propagandists would enlist his services. His activities might be directed toward getting some hip-hop schoolman into an educational office or in preventing such a pedagogue from being deservingly dismissed; in having local authorities change their methods; and in persuading school officials to take up doubtful innovations that for the moment might have the support of the secretary or those giving him counsel.

Frequently the statement has been made by those advocating the measure that a department of education is essential in order that all existing educational projects of the Federal government may be consolidated and put under common direction. They freely assert that present educational activities sponsored by various Federal departments lack definite purpose and efficiency. Also they condemn governmental officials for prescribing the course of study to be followed under certain Federal aid as well as the tendency of Federal field agents to become a source of interference with local school systems. But no one has reason to expect anything else from departments supported by congressional appropriations and administered by presidential appointees whose first concern is to serve the appointing power. Relief from such conditions certainly would not come through placing all these activities in the hands of one individual who could be controlled so much more easily by his political master. The most pressing need is for schoolmen throughout the country to assume the position that any Federal aid with strings tied to it will be rejected—and that of all possible strings the least acceptable would be some mediocre pedagogue parading about the land as the king-pin of education "by presidential appointment."

IX

The case against the proposed department may be permitted to rest here. If Ichabod wants a portfolio, let him cease masquerading as an educator and go in for straight politics.

That educational research may accomplish much in the United States in the future is not questioned, but there is reason for insisting that it shall not be entrusted to a highly financed Federal department, or even that such a department should become the clearing house for the research carried on by independent school systems and professional groups.

That a different type of leadership is desirable may be admitted, and coupled to it, the assertion that if it is to have any real merit it must be unlike the sort of leadership sponsored by those groups that are now shouting for the department. These groups have carried leadership almost to the goal which might be attained through basing it on a cabinet portfolio—complete politicalization. A department of education, with its secretary in the President's cabinet, will certainly not bring about the quality of leadership which public education requires; most likely it would prove a serious, possibly an insurmountable, obstacle in the way of developing the kind of educational leadership that will be of real worth to democracy.

CHAPTER IV

MORE MONEY FOR LESS EDUCATION

But America Is Young and Rich

I

America today is spending a lot of money on public education. But as the years roll by, the annual expenditures will inevitably roll up, so that the 1929 burden may be regarded as relatively light compared to what the people must shoulder eventually. My purpose here is neither to proffer consolation to the taxpayer, except as he can find it in the assurance that the worst is yet to come, nor to point out ways of escape, since there are none. Rather, I aim only to explain how costliness came to be the ideal of American education, and, somewhat sadly perhaps, to bear witness to the superbly diligent manner in which the schools at present are pursuing that ideal.

It is common knowledge that school costs have gone up by leaps and bounds. Without causing a ripple of excitement, George D. Strayer, professor of educational administration at Teachers College (Columbia), could testify before a recent Southern Conference on Education that in 1926 the United States spent approximately

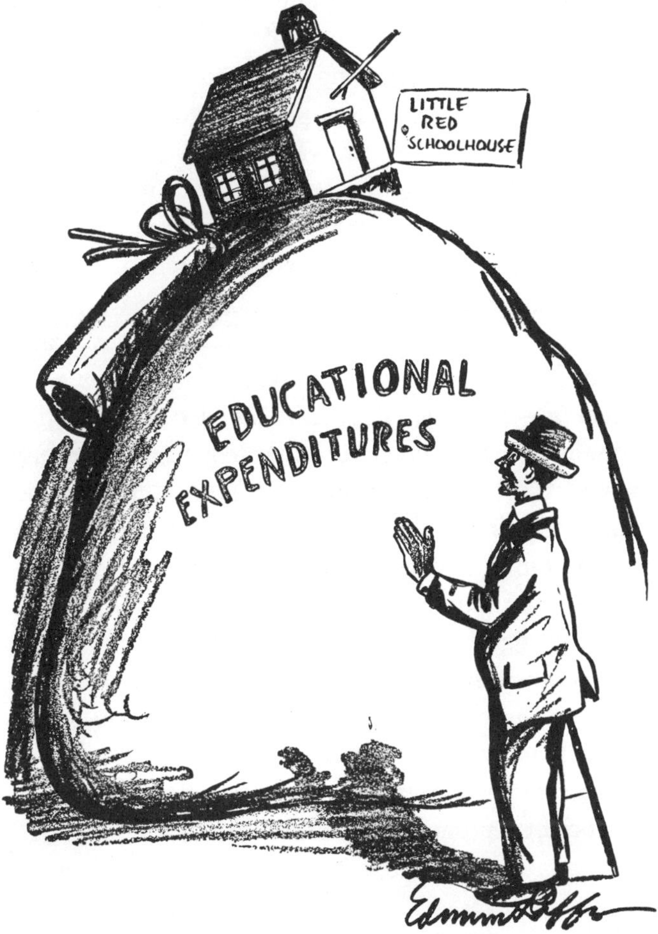
LITTLE
RED
SCHOOLHOUSE
EDUCATIONAL
EXPENDITURES

four times as much for its public schools as it spent in 1910, and then added: "The end of this upward scale *is not in sight.*" Regarding the increases already recorded, I shall, in due course, present figures which will show that Doctor Strayer was, if anything, too conservative. As to the future, time will undoubtedly prove him right—provided, of course, that the shock of swallowing the rapidly increasing school budgets does not kill the goose which lays the golden eggs.

The forward-lookers in education, who now completely dominate their craft, recognize but one measure of success—quantity. They have adopted the yardstick of the commercial go-getter as their gauge, and refuse to see any evidence of progress save mere bigness. Worse, they have managed to force this criterion upon their customer and victim, the taxpayer. Ask him, in any average American town, whether his community is progressing educationally, and he will answer affirmatively only if he can quote a phenomenal rise, year after year, in school costs. He has been educated by the educators to assume that any system which spends, say, 30 per cent more this year than last offers irrefutable evidence of a progressive and idealistic spirit.

II

Perhaps it was Leonard P. Ayres, at the time with the Russell Sage Foundation, who gave the first great boost to this new practice of evaluating school systems quantitatively. In his book, *An Index Number for State School Systems,* published in 1920, he calculated the worth of each State's educational system by taking account of ten factors, five having to do with the quantitative aspect of attendance and five dealing with the amount of expenditures.

His ratings by this ingenious procedure, for some unknown reason, were straightway accepted as fair and plausible, and thus was blazed a new path to success in school administration. No need thereafter for superintendents to bother about such elusive matters as the quality of the instruction given nor the manner in which it might function later. Professional success could be computed, quickly and precisely, by noting the increasing fruitfulness of the superintendent's annual raids on the public exchequer. Today an American schoolman, called on to render an account of his stewardship, almost invariably begins—and ends—by pointing to pretentious buildings and obese budgets. He is willing to stand or fall by his ability to make the people spend more money.

But before I attempt a survey of the means by which the cost of public education has been thus increased, it may be well to show exactly what the rate of increase has been. Professor Strayer, on the occasion mentioned, compared the school costs in 1926 with those of 1910 and stated that expenditures had quadrupled, going from approximately $500,000,000 to approximately

$2,000,000,000. As always, he was too modest in telling what the leaders in school administration had done for the taxpayer. The actual bill for public schools in 1910 was $426,250,434; by 1926 it had mounted to $2,026,308,190. Four times the 1910 cost would be $1,705,001,736; so that the Professor, in his modesty, overlooked the trifling sum of $321,306,454!

But why use the figures of 1910 for a comparison? They tell only the end of the story. The records of 1900 are much more illuminating. For example:

TABLE I

	1900	1926	Increase
Pupils enrolled................	15,503,110	24,741,468	59%
Teachers employed.............	423,062	814,169	90%
Salaries paid..................	$137,687,746	$1,100,316,674	700%
New buildings and equipment....	35,450,820	411,037,774	1050%
Expenditures for other purposes..	41,826,052	514,953,742	1130%

III

Naturally, the taxpayer may wonder how the schoolmen have been able to sustain such stupendous rates of increase. I admit it has been a big job. Of course, the dollar lost something of its purchasing power between 1900 and 1926, and to whatever extent this is reflected in the higher cost of the public schools the schoolmen claim no credit, no more than would a housewife pride herself on paying twice as much today for a steak as she gave in 1900. But after allowing everything for the depreciation of the dollar, more than enough remains to cover with glory all those schoolmen who have practiced so triumphantly the gentle art of what they are pleased to call "creative administration."

The master stroke in starting school expenditures skyward consisted in staging an endless race between all the American school systems to see which one, in any year, could make the highest record of expenditures. When this competition was inaugurated, each superintendent had as the nucleus about which to erect his administration of costliness an educational unit which had for long been engaged in teaching more or less fundamental things as efficiently and economically as possible. But efficiency and economy could have no place in an educational progress measured exclusively by expenditures, and so radical treatment had to be administered to alter the inherited units.

It was no boy's job which the forward-looking schoolmen tackled when they started to knock efficiency, economy, and the fundamentals into a cocked hat. The American people thought they had grown great and prosperous through practicing economy and efficiency, and were not easily to be persuaded that it was proper to employ their wealth for the purpose of establishing a reign of inefficiency and prodigality in their public schools. Again, teaching the fundamentals had tradition back of it, and some people, a bit old-fashioned perhaps, were disposed to demand the continued teaching of them, even after the bars had been let down for certain new fads and frills. But the trick of winning over this lay population was swiftly and effectively turned by the schoolmen when they instigated a rivalry among all the systems to see which could blow the school budget biggest—in other words, when they turned the prevailing go-getterism to the uses of pedagogy.

Observe how the thing worked. The opulent Babbitt of, say, the city of X (whose offspring, if he had such encumbrances, attended private schools) would never have responded on altruistic grounds to a proposal that he bear a tax rate which would permit the X's common schools to surpass in costliness of maintenance the most exclusive private institutions. But when this idealistic butter-and-egg man was told that in this matter, the city of X was competing with Chicago, Pittsburgh, Los Angeles, and like cities, each bent upon seeing which could make public education cost most, his sporting blood warmed up. Soon he was not only ready to approve the budget in hand—he was demanding that the school officials find new and costly features to tag on to it. It was imperative, he felt, that his city be recognized as the most progressive, educationally, in the country. That, he believed, was good advertising for X, and, incidentally, for his butter-and-egg business.

There is something sublimely American about the spirit with which various cities have entered this contest for supremacy in the costliness of their school buildings; the salaries paid their school officials and, to a smaller degree, their teachers; and the number of luxurious fads included in their school programs. A single illustration will show how perfectly the thing works in practice: A certain city contemplates erecting a new high school. Under the old style of school administration, the substantial citizens of the community would have sought facts by asking such questions as: Is a new building actually needed? What student body will it have to accommodate? How much can the town afford to spend? What type of structure will best serve the purposes for which this school is intended? Will it be both efficient and economical? But under the new spell of inter-system rivalry, an entirely different type of information is sought. School officials scour the country for the big "show" high schools. Details are tabulated concerning size, style, equipment, extras, and especially cost. This dope is turned over to the architect with instructions to create something that will make all existing high schools look like thirty cents—and he does it.

As a device for increasing the cost of public education, this rivalry is almost perfect. Witness how the annual bill for schoolhouses and equipment rose 1050 per cent in a quarter of a century, while school expenditures for "other purposes," which largely cover the high cost of operating the new plants, jumped 1130 per cent in the same period, although the student population scored only a 59 per cent gain.

IV

But the forward-looking schoolman has not been so shortsighted as to put all his eggs into one basket. While developing his scheme for putting each system's building program into competition with the program of all other systems, so as to make public education costlier, he has also given profound thought to the possibilities of the payroll. He could, of course, expand the salary item on the budget by periodically increasing the pay for all school positions, including his own. He has done this, in fact—by diligently keeping his community fully informed about what other systems were doing in the matter of raising salaries. But increasing the pay of existing functionaries did not, by itself, produce as quick results as were demanded by educational "progress." Therefore the payroll was subjected simultaneously to both a front and a rear attack. At the same time that the average of teachers' salaries was being raised 296 per cent, during the period 1900-1926, the army of teachers drawing this steadily increasing wage was expanded 90 per cent.

What to do with the additional teachers was a problem. A simple solution would have been to put them on the payroll and then send them into the parks for sunning. But such a method would have missed the service these newcomers could render, outside the pay they drew, in making education cost more. Therefore, new types of activity had to be devised. All kinds of fads, many of them exquisitely futile, were grafted on to the public-school system and piped to the public exchequer. Of course, all these innovations appealed strongly to the big butter-and-egg man, once he had been won, heart and soul, to the side of educational "progress." Just as he likes to boast that every new automobile contrivance, no matter how senseless, is put on his cars the instant it becomes available, so, having caught the fever of inter-system rivalry, he insists that the school officials in his home town be constantly on the lookout for the very latest novelties in education. If the local superintendent chances to be in a town which is entertaining Colonel Lindbergh, and instantly telegraphs his home papers that he proposes to start a course in aviation as part of the elementary curriculum, he is hailed by the butter-and-egg man as a truly progressive administrator. Thus, any project that promises to be costly and futile finds the latchstring of the up-to-date school system hanging out for it.

The champions of these new fads, of course, do not take kindly to those who still believe in the old-fashioned fundamentals. But this difficulty may be smoothed over by prohibiting the teaching of the fundamentals in really "progressive" schools. Evidence of such a trend is seen in the costlier private elementary schools of the so-called experimental type, where the fundamentals are treated like unloved stepchildren; while a parent who dares complain because his offspring is not learning to read, write, and cipher, is treated like a bigamistic stepfather. These institutions are already being copied, with fair success, by tax-supported schools. I could name certain public schools wherein the primary teachers boldly assert that they are engaged to encourage the "natural development" of the child through a "socialized" school atmosphere, and announce that they do not propose to stoop to teaching reading and the multiplication tables.

By expanding the field of the public schools horizontally through adding all the new fads, and by elaborating the supervisory side, an opportunity has been afforded the progressive schoolman to create many new and highly remunerative positions. Prior to 1900, educators were cautious about building any formidable organization outside the force of classroom teachers. At present, however, the smallest system, if ambitious to rank well, senses the need of an elaborate bureaucracy around the administrative office. The process of such elaboration has been standardized. An individual is hired as an expert in a specialized field. As soon as he finds a place to hang his hat and a desk whereon to prop his feet he begins dreaming of expansion. If only he can arrange to get a few assistants, he may convert his office into a department, and his own appellation into that of director. He consults the more-money-for-education superintendent, and discovers that the thing can be arranged. Thus there blossoms forth a department with a director, supervisors, assistants, and a budget.

There is no end to the activities that justify such departments in a system which is ambitious to spend money — vocational education, vocational guidance, manual training, Americanization, educational research, curriculum study, tests and measurements, mental hygiene, physical education, home economics, domestic science, music, art, continuation schools, evening schools, summer schools, playground activities, kindergartens, primary education, intermediate grades, junior high schools, high schools, special classes, etc. To maintain the rate of growth each such unit will soon or late place within every school building a representative who will be part of the special department or bureau rather than of the particular school or of the system as a whole.

In the present day, more than ever before, it should be possible for the American people, educators and laymen, to discuss school costs calmly and sensibly. However, it is becoming increasingly difficult for any one who looks at a school budget critically to get a decent hearing. This difficulty results from the lordly attitude assumed by most proponents of more money for education. Perhaps they have sense enough to know the weakness of their position and think to interfere with those who might expose that weakness. Their trick is an application of the old legal maxim: When you have no case, abuse your opponent—and they resort to abuse.

The basis for most of the criticism in this book of school expenditures is the refusal of those who demand more money for education to justify their demands. Certainly the writer is not against spending state funds for public education, even up to many times the amount now being paid out, provided the school people can justify the spending of every dollar they ask. But instead they make an effort to obscure the issue by dragging in irrelevant matters, as, for instance, the amount of money now being paid out for tobacco, automobiles, and cosmetics.

These same schoolmen would be the first to condemn any other public official who adopted a like practice. Fancy a superintendent of public lighting, when he makes up his annual budget, arbitrarily demanding that the amount of money allowed him be in proportion to the funds alloted to the engineer in charge of public highways. His case properly is rested upon certain facts: the extent of the territory to be lighted; the volume of illumination required; the cost of electricity and gas. But the *last word* in defense of increased school expenditures, a recently published bulletin of the National Education Association,[1] shows different tactics.

The layman has a right to assume that when great research specialists in this organization undertake to prepare material to be used in combating public criticism of school costs, they will reveal at least a trace of wisdom and some originality. However, the layman will find here merely silly, stereotyped arguments that carry no conviction. Now for a few samples from the sixty-page booklet:

The most reliable estimate of the income of the people of the United States is that of the National Bureau of Economic Research. According to this agency, the incomes of all the people of the United States added together amounted to $89,419,000,000 in 1928, the last year for which there are figures. In the same year, according to the United States Office of Education, we expended $2,448,633,561 for public schools. . . . Since we had an income of $89,419,-000,000 and expended $2,448,633,561 for public schools, 2.74 per cent of our income went for their support. . . .

The nation's bill for life insurance in 1928 was $3,145,-584,000. This figure may be compared with $2,448,633,561 expended for public schools of all types—elementary, secondary, collegiate. The nation's annual bill for life insurance is, therefore, considerably larger than that paid for public education. Out of every $100 which we have to

---

[1] *Investing in Public Education.* Research Bulletin of the National Education Association, Volume VIII, No. 4, September, 1930.

spend, we pay $2.74 for public schools and $3.52 for life insurance premiums. . . .

In 1928 there were 21,379,125 passenger automobiles in operation in the United States. We own 77 per cent of all the automobiles of the world. Excluding motor trucks from consideration, we expended in 1928 approximately $12,500,000,000 for the purchase, operation, and upkeep of passenger automobiles.

The public school bill represents an investment of $2.74 out of each $100 of income; the passenger automobile bill claims $13.98 out of each $100 of income. Do these facts indicate that public school expenditures represent an overvaluation of the importance of education? . . .

Our luxury bill far exceeds that for all public schools. [The research experts work out approximations for the cost of tobacco; soft drinks, ice cream, candy, and chewing gum; theaters, movies, and similar amusements; jewelry, perfumes, and cosmetics; sporting goods, toys, etc., although to make the next paragraph more impressive many of these items are omitted.] For every $1.00 spent for schools, $2.61 is spent for candy, chewing gum, theaters, and similar items. Do these facts indicate that we overvalue education—that we invest more in the education of our children than we can afford?

Now such bunk—and there is lots more of it—does not even come within hailing distance of the demand that public education justify its expenditures, nor does it give the impression that a clear-cut justification is possible without a far more penetrating study of the problem. The American people may be spending too much or too little for chewing gum. Even if these research experts should be able to determine just how much should go for this commodity, their findings would have no value in calculating how much should be spent on education. Again, the income of a people does not necessarily serve as a reliable basis for determining how much should be paid for education. The Bulletin points out the percentage of the income in each State that is devoted to the schools. The average for the country is $2.74 out of the $100. We find Florida spending 5.76 per cent of the incomes in the State; on the other side of the scale is Maine with 1.93 per cent; Maryland, with 1.97 per cent; and Massachusetts, with 1.85 per cent. To any one who knows the quality of public education in these several States, the data presented make absolutely ridiculous the suggestion that it is possible to decide what percentage of the people's incomes may be required to provide adequate and efficient schools.

Finally, the authors of the Bulletin innocently offer testimony against their own position, which is to justify the increased expenditures for schools. To quote:

Why does the comparatively small bill which the public pays for the education of children attract so much attention, while much larger bills paid for privately purchased items attract so little attention? . . . The taxpayer's contact with the school is not close. He thinks of schooling in terms of the obsolete institutions he attended a generation ago. . . .

Our yearly national income now approaches ninety billion dollars. That this income is ninety billions, rather than fifty or sixty, is very largely due to human factors, special capacities possessed by the nation's citizenry, which are the result of such agencies as good schools. These qualities have not been developed in a day or a decade. To the extent that they are an outcome of schooling, they are the product of many decades. The creation of a superior culture in any direction is the work of many generations. The nation since its beginning has maintained educational facilities so that an increasing per cent of the population might have opportunities to develop its potentialities. The fruit of this devotion to education is now being harvested.

Before passing on, note here the inconsistency of the defendants of an unjustified increase in school expenditures. First, they assert that the taxpayer may be disposed to protest, since he was schooled in an obsolete institution. In their next breath they give credit to the products of those same obsolete institutions for practically all that we are today.

V

Having thus glanced at a few of the means employed by "creative administration" to make public education cost more, one may ask: Will these things be sufficient to maintain the present rate of yearly increase in school costs? Not by a jug-full! More schemes must be devised—ever more and more. Thus it is a gigantic task which confronts the educational forward-looker. The total expenditures for public schools jumped from

$214,964,618 in 1900 to $1,946,096,912 in 1925. If this rate of increase—ninefold in exactly twenty-five years—is to be duplicated during the second quarter of the century, then for the year 1950 the schools must be able to consume $17,514,872,208 of public money. We must not forget, however, that there was a depreciation in the buying power of the dollar during the first quarter of the century. If this is not duplicated during 1925-1950, then instead of being required to spend seventeen billions in 1950, school officials may be called on to develop their programs so as to find outlets for less than this. However, to find ways for spending even ten or twelve billion dollars in a year will demand considerable ingenuity.

Let us take account of the size of the job. Suppose a newly-rich chain-store proprietor instructs a caterer to furnish for him a banquet which will surpass anything ever before put on. A caterer of imagination should be able to accommodate him. But if this same newly-rich comes back, time and time again, and on each occasion insists that the next affair make the one immediately preceding appear, by comparison, tame and cheap, the caterer will have the real task; all the chain-store Croesus will have to do will be to pay the bills. There is a similarity between this hypothetical situation and the actual case of the "progressive" schoolman and the public. The people have merely to provide the funds for meeting the increasing expenditures, but the unfortunate schoolman must rack his brains to devise new means for making education cost more.

So far, this discussion has been concerned chiefly with what is being done by the educational caterer in the matter of the elementary and secondary schools; but it is unreasonable to expect these two parts of the public school system to bear the whole burden of making education costlier. Therefore, most wisely, forward-looking educators are already engaged in building the public schools up into the life of the adult, so that eventually his education at the public expense will stop only when he dies. And at the same time the system is being built down into the nursery in order that the new-born child of tomorrow will literally tumble into a classroom.

No need here to rehearse what is being done even now by the state-supported colleges and universities. Occasionally a bilious individual, out of tune with the ideals of progressive education, undertakes to criticize them for their alleged sins of omission and commission. But a glance at their budgets discloses the fact that practically all of them are doing their share to make public education cost more. What if they do take all sorts and conditions of youths, wrestling with the question of what to do in life, and arbitrarily assign them to courses which give them neither pleasure nor profit, and then turn them out, after four or more years, with their ability to wrestle with their original problem somewhat reduced?

Simply on the score of conformity with the latest purpose of making education costlier, such a course is now regarded as commendable. We should not forget that these higher institutions have accepted responsibility of training students, not only for the vocations and professions, but for leisure as well. When a liberal arts college in a state university takes in hundreds of students, year after year, for the purpose of preparing them better to fit into American life, and then turns them loose, as graduates, equipped only with a few fragments of useless knowledge, its aim doubtless is to train them for leisure, even though it be that of the hobo.

VI

What is really needed is that the production of graduates be speeded up. The coming of the junior college, taking just two years to make a full-fledged college man, should give considerable help here. All sorts of junior colleges can be established, at the public expense, to offer vocational training of an elementary type and confer dignified degrees. The possibilities here have been already scented. G. Vernon Bennett, of the University of Southern California, in *Vocational Education of Junior College Grade,* indicates what may be done in this line to increase the nation's expenditures for public education. In collaboration with a group of teachers interested in vocational education, he compiled a tentative list of the vocations for which training could be offered by state-supported junior colleges. This group decided that such callings as those of the café manager, the automobile salesman, the detective, the dressmaker, the railway-station agent, the storekeeper, the upholsterer, the traveling salesman, the hotel keeper, and the undertaker should be regarded as of junior-college grade.

An exhaustive study was made of twenty-eight occupations accorded this grading, and it was found that, in order to keep that limited number supplied with graduates, 471,000 students should be kept in training, producing an annual crop of 189,626 graduates. By this scheme the country would be able to spend $143,000,000 more money annually on public education. Professor Bennett, it will be observed, took account of but twenty-eight vocations out of more than one hundred that might be regarded as of junior-college grade. Moreover, there is no reason why thousands of colleges of slightly lower rank might not be created, out of the public funds, for training manicurists, collectors for instalment houses, grocery clerks, waitresses, doorkeepers and flunkies for movie theatres, and the like.

Again, there is the rapidly developing project of adult education. This newcomer in the pedagogical grove is peculiarly appealing, for, on the more or less sound theory that "once an adult, always an adult," the taxpayers may at one clip acquire the burden of educating millions upon millions of lifetime students.

There is little tradition back of the enterprise; therefore educators may use their imaginations freely. Frankly, I know nothing about the subject myself. Some months back, the literary editor of *The Nation* assigned me the task of reviewing the first six volumes on adult education to be published in America. I read them all, not because I am a conscientious reviewer, but because I hoped to pick up information. My net gain from this exhaustive reading was a suggestion, made by Alfred Lawrence Hall-Quest in *The University Afield,* that when we think about adult education, we should recognize certain existing agencies already at work, such as the Y. M. C. A., the Y. W. C. A., the chautauquas and lyceums, the public libraries, and the museums.

Whether adult education is merely deferred elementary education, as in the case of illiterates, or the application of a high cultural polish, such as might be gained by sitting at the feet of a typical congressman when he lectures—this, after all, is an academic question that will not be allowed to retard the growth of the movement. Almost anything imaginable could be included in its province—teaching old women bridge, bankers the game of golf, nursemaids the technique of horseback riding, and flappers the art of crossing their legs.

There are so many possibilities in adult education, such unlimited opportunities for spending public money, that the taxpayer naturally is for it—strong.

VII

Public education is soon going to cost more in another way—and here scarcely the beginning is in sight. That is, through building a magnificent substructure beneath the primary grades. Not so many years back, educators debated seriously whether the schools should admit pupils at five or six years of age. Tightwad economy complexioned the discussion. But economy has since been cast to the wind, and the schools are ready to tackle the child while it is still an infant. According to a circular being distributed by the Maryland Association for Kindergarten Extension:

The early years of childhood are today receiving the attention of American psychologists from New England to California. Clinics and laboratories for the observation of children from birth to six years of age have been established in most of our great universities. Why? Because psychologists realize that these years are the formative years of life; because they see in them the seed time from which the fruition of later years is to follow. Upon this new knowledge and understanding is being built a new education, which begins at the cradle. It provides a nursery school as a supplement to the home for the children from two to four.

Since the primary aim is to make education cost

more, is there any sound reason why educators should arbitrarily select the age of two years as the time when the public treasury will begin educating the child? The start in fact could be made much sooner. John B. Watson, formerly professor of psychology at Johns Hopkins University, addressing a group of women recently, made the point that what is done with the child long before it reaches two, indeed while it is still the tiniest infant, may decide whether it is to be another Beethoven or just another shoemaker. Perhaps the first two years are really the important ones, since, according to Doctor Watson, all habits and reactions can be "built in" to the child while it is living these first years.

Just so soon as a technique for this "building in" has been developed by the behaviorists, the American public schools will begin to specialize in the production of geniuses, provided, of course, enough pupils can be saved from the corrupting influence of mother love. The home, we are told, is not able to assume responsibility for training the child even during its first years, and so the job must be shifted to the teachers. However, I suspect that no need will be found to discontinue the present courses for training adolescent girls and young women for married life and motherhood. Even though they will not be permitted to employ the knowledge gained from such courses, the courses themselves will remain useful, for they will make public education costly.

But let us go back to the preschool child. The leader of the forward-lookers here is Miss Patty Smith Hill, professor of kindergarten education at Teachers College (Columbia). While mere male educators are dabbling with picayune schemes which increase school costs 50 per cent or 100 per cent a year, Miss Hill has prepared a program which, almost over night, could carry our annual expenditures to the eight billion mark. America deserves the note of rebuke with which Miss Hill opens her article, "Preschool Education as a Career," in *The Journal of the National Education Association:*

Very young children have just as much right to all those influences which make for maximum growth as any later stage of development, yet the state is slow to grant this. Maximum growth at any stage of development demands an environment equipped to stimulate developing powers plus a highly trained guide to utilize these facilities to produce achievement of a high order. . . .

We are not fully civilized today. Boards of education all over the land refuse a tax for preschool children, leaving them to chance, for better or worse, in homes with untrained mothers, or in the streets with no supervision. It is only recently that a tax was procurable for education of children from four to six years of age and the battle is yet to be fought for the nursery-school child.

A new day is dawning. We are asking and demanding our right to a professional preparation commensurate with opportunities offered those in the upper grades and secondary schools. We are also invading the homes of the present and future, insisting on parental and preparental training of mothers, and shall we venture to say fathers, as well?

VIII

Not only will the public, tax-supported nursery-schools of the future provide for all such infants as may be voluntarily brought to them; champions of the new baby-schools hint that their group will not hesitate to invade the home and literally cart off the youngsters. If, in the next twenty-five years, such baby schools are established in sufficient number to provide for all babies, then there is no question about the stupendous educational progress, measured by dollars, which this suffering nation is destined to make. Here are Miss Hill's plans:

There is a periodical examination far more thorough and superior in every way to those offered by schools of any type in the past; there is the daily inspection given by trained nurses before the child is allowed to join his playmates; there is the daily régime of scientific feeding, sleep, rest, and open air work and play; there is a psychological and psychiatric clinic with its mental, emotional, and social diagnosis; there is the daily record kept by the nursery-school teacher herself which, when put together with the findings of doctors, nurses, psychologists, psychiatrists, nutritionists, dentists, posture experts, and case workers, give as full a clinical study or picture of the child's whole personality as is possible to secure. In addition to records made in the nursery, a home report is brought daily by the mother with a record of the child's home sleep, both as to quality and quantity, the appetite, elimination, emotional disturbances, and open air opportunities. Parental coöperation is required as a condition of entrance and the education of the mother is considered an integral part of nursery education.

Parents, no doubt, will willingly comply with all these requirements, for they will realize that no royal prince ever enjoyed, since he could not afford it, the kind of nursery care the taxpayers of America will accord all its babies—white, black, yellow, and mixed. Here we see the type of pedagogue who will teach baby:

The nursery-school teacher must have some of the knowledge and skill of the trained nurse, together with the attitude and ability of a wise, intelligent mother, since she takes over many of the duties which only trained nurses and mothers in the past were supposed to be willing or prepared to do for little children. Nothing that the child needs can be regarded as menial by a thoroughly trained nursery teacher. She must have a goodly share of the medical knowledge which pediatricians are supposed to possess. She must be well inducted into the intricacies of psychiatry or mental hygiene and skillful in the use of such knowledge in meeting the emotional disturbances and behavior problems of child life. She must be prepared to enter intelligently into the nutritional program mapped out by experts in this field. She must be an expert in teaching correct habits of sleep and posture. In addition to such knowledge and skills, not usually possessed by teachers, the nursery teacher must have a full knowledge of the relation of her curriculum to those in kindergarten and primary education, with their literature, art, music, games, dances, and social studies as carried forward in modern education.

What a soul-inspiring picture! Could any red-blooded American refuse to pay taxes until it hurts and, if need be, hock his shirt, that the humblest child hereafter born in America may be started aright in life in such a nursery school? What food for the idealistic imagination! Let's have just one nibble.

A tiny tot is carried by its mother to the door of the baby school. There the mother surrenders her offspring to the receiving official, together with a detailed report of its life since the closing hour of the preceding day. The receiving official conveys the baby to the studio of the trained nurses, where it is thoroughly inspected before being permitted to join its playmates. During this inspection a nurse, inadvertently, jabs a finger in baby's eye and it begins to bellow. It is rushed posthaste to the psychiatric section to have its emotion interpreted. A psychiatrist tickles it under the chin with the left hind leg of a graveyard rabbit, and the youngster responds by smiling, whereupon the learned gentleman announces that it has been restored to a proper mental state for mingling with its playmates. Then a thoroughly trained nursery teacher leads it into the spacious school gardens, where, in the open air, it can play on the sand pile.

The little tot surveys its playmates; glances at the thoroughly trained nursery teachers who form a fringe around the group of pupils, scrutinizes the palatial structure to which it will shortly be escorted for scientific feeding and scientific rest, and then, just to prove that out of the mouths of babes and sucklings occasionally may come a word of wisdom, says—*Boloney!*

CHAPTER V

THE POOR ENRICHED CURRICULUM

A Triumph for the Progressives

I

When placed with a stranger at a small table of a railway diner, an effort to ignore this other traveler, whose dishes are continually colliding with yours, becomes more burdensome than listening to his conversation, no matter how trite. Consequently, on this particular occasion I smiled an assent for the man opposite me to open up, and he began to talk schools.

He was a clean-cut, intelligent fellow, with the front of a broker, the enthusiasm of a baseball fan, and more common sense than average broker and fan combined. He had gone into education because the vocation appealed to him, and his experience had not cooled his professional ardor. From a modest teaching position he had advanced to an administrative office where he devoted his efforts primarily to vocational education.

This teacher, talking his stuff, dwelt upon the rosy outlook in a country where youths apparently are eager to grasp the wonderful educational opportunities open to them. His school system conducts numerous evening classes where boys and girls who work by day find it possible to supplement such education as they may have acquired before being permitted to seek remunerative employment. He spoke feelingly of lads of sixteen to twenty, some working as messengers and delivery boys, who were attending night school so as to prepare themselves for better jobs.

Hard-boiled as I am, the recital thrilled. What a picture! Fine young fellows, who had quit school early on account of economic pressure, toiling at menial vocations during the day, but resisting the temptation to idle away their evenings and, instead, attending night school. I could fancy ambition prompting one to take up accountancy or banking, another to study mechanical drawing and engineering, a third going in for chemistry or law. And then, for my own information, I asked what subjects were most commonly taken by these youths.

"Arithmetic, composition, penmanship."

"High school work?"

"Oh, no! elementary."

"Surely not elementary arithmetic and English?"

"Yes"—and he seemed disturbed by my tone.

"In other words, when working boys who have already attended day school for the prescribed number of years come to your night classes, you offer them the same sort of elementary training that should have been acquired in the early intermediate grades?"

"But they are not sufficiently advanced for anything else," he apologized.

"In that case, I'll allow you are doing a fine work. If boys who are required by law to attend school until their fourteenth year, on going out to gain a living find that they have not got a common school training, then it's a wonderful thing for you, with the aid of Smith and Hughes, to remove the deficiency, instead of attempting to teach them boxing, civics, and parliamentary law."

II

This leads to the hypothetical case of one Sam Jones, a bundle boy. He attended public school from his fifth year, when he was admitted to the kindergarten, until at fourteen he simultaneously completed the prescribed work of the junior high school and escaped jurisdiction of the compulsory-attendance law. These ten years of school attendance presumably were filled with activity —if not in the matter of acquiring the old-fashioned fundamentals, at least in educational pursuits of importance in qualifying him to meet such conditions as confront the average wage earner. The question is, What were these pursuits?

The Jones boy could be quizzed about what was done for him during the years he spent in school, but he might be forgetful, or prejudiced, or perhaps not able to comprehend the big purpose that lay behind the daily program. The simpler course, then, is to ascertain what goals may have been set by those pedagogues whom the State paid to educate him. These goals should be indicated in the manual prepared by supervisors and others for the guidance of classroom teachers. The course of study of any system might be expected to reveal what things the classroom instructor is required to teach, what attainments the pupil is expected to register at various grade levels, and approved procedures.

What follows is an attempt to present a bird's-eye view of the teacher's job as it might appear to a beginning teacher after having studied the course of study prepared for his guidance. The material represents a composite of abstracts from the courses of two city systems[1] that have won often deserved preëminence as propagators of Progressive education. It indicates aims, subject matter, and approved activities.

III

At the outset, for the orientation of those who will deal with young children, a word is said about the importance of permitting the child to direct his own

[1] Los Angeles City School District Course of Study. Kindergarten. First and Second Grades. Third and Fourth Grades. Fifth and Sixth Grades. Syllabus for Seventh and Eighth Grades. Los Angeles, Calif., 1924, 1925, 1926.

Board of Education of the City of St. Louis. Curriculum Bulletins No. 5, No. 9, No. 11, No. 13, No. 21. St. Louis, Mo., 1926.

education through pursuing such caprices as may sprout in his young mind:

For many years courses of study have been outlined wholly in terms of subjects. Today there is a growing tendency to state the curriculum in terms of the child's activities and interests. . . . It is evident that an activity with elements closely interwoven—one which is an evolution of a simple play need to a more and more elaborate scheme—will not admit of outside interference without setting aside the child's plan, confusing him or even discouraging the completion of the task. What, then, is the teacher's responsibility toward such a unit of activity? The most she can do is to provide an environment favorable to expansion, and direct the scheme with subtle suggestion or question into even more productive and social channels. She plans to have more materials accessible, more toys, dolls, clay, paint, lumber, scraps, room, music, books, paper, conversation, and motives.[1]

It is not enough, however, for the teacher to stock the classroom like a toyshop lest, when the youngsters go out-of-doors, they be confronted with the perilous situation of having to romp about or play some silly old-fashioned game as catchers or leapfrog.

Where playground room permits, little children can do much with boards, boxes, old auto tires, ropes, trees, fences, steps, kegs, sidewalks, gravel, bricks, rocks, shells, broken crockery, and nature materials.[2]

[1] Los Angeles, op. cit.
[2] Los Angeles, op. cit.

But a teacher, thinking to take his class out-of-doors, may be disturbed concerning the manner in which some of these suggestions are to be executed. For instance, is he to trespass upon private property in quest of fences and steps, trees and sidewalks, and to what extent may he take the hazard of placing broken crockery in the hands of young children. Less disturbing is the suggestion:

Have the kindergarten children participate in the following activities—

> Walking to market
> Looking at the front of buildings or stores
> Looking at the arrangement of doors and windows
> Looking at the arrangement of the interior
> Looking at the arrangement of articles on shelves.[1]

At this level pupils are expected to show evidence of such accomplishments as—

> The habit of using the mirror[2]
> Creating and learning a prayer.[3]

IV

If the pupil acquires a proper mind-set in the kindergarten, he need experience no jar when advanced to the first grade. Having become adept at that early age in gazing at buildings and displayed

---
[1] St. Louis, op. cit.
[2] Los Angeles, op. cit.
[3] St. Louis, op. cit.

merchandise, he is prepared for more momentous social ventures, such as:

The class may take a walk to the nearest home represented, calling on the mother or baby.[1]

There is a possibility, of course, that the mother of a child in the first grade, who has an even younger offspring at home demanding such attention as can be spared from household duties, will be so delighted in having the class drop in on her without warning, that she will speed the departing guests. In this contingency the teacher can avail himself of the suggestion that the class go into the garden to see the chickens, rabbits, or flowers. On their way back to school "the pupils may observe a vegetable wagon and question the driver."

The training in social graces given first-grade pupils is bound to be noted and appreciated by the folks at home. The teacher is to train the young children to:

Use tableware, dishes, spoons, knife, and napkin.
Cut food.
Eat all of serving.
Enjoy attractive service, to comment on it.
Lace shoes, button dress and waist.
Use toilet.
Recognize and name correctly tissue paper.[2]

Moreover, in order that the ties between school and home may be strengthened, the pupils are to bring

[1] Los Angeles, op. cit.
[2] Los Angeles, op. cit.

wagons, bicycles, kiddie cars, etc., to school; decorate them and arrange a parade. At the same time the pupil is to be started on his way of making useful things during school hours. Here is a model activity:

One morning a supervisor entered a first grade room wearing a bouquet of worsted flowers on her coat. The children admired it very much and upon being told that the flowers had been made by children in another first grade, asked if they too might make some. Christmas was drawing near and all agreed that mother must have the flowers as a trimming for her hat. Many thought they could make extra ones for grandmother and for other members of the family. . . .

Upon stepping into the room the week before Christmas, one could have seen forty happy children with a bouquet carefully wrapped in tissue paper and placed in a small box which they had also made, ready to be taken home for mother's Christmas.[1]

Poetic license does not apply to so serious a discussion as that under way, and therefore no attempt will be made to picture the forty happy mothers as they go forth on Christmas morn resplendent in their winter bonnets trimmed with these beautiful worsted flowers.

When the pupil reaches the second grade another type of social activity is appropriate:

The pupils may participate in a group activity which will provide pleasure for others—making kites. Discuss the ma-

[1] Los Angeles, op. cit.

THE POOR ENRICHED CURRICULUM 95

terials needed for making kites. Have the children plan to secure those which are not supplied. Have the children invite another class to the kiteflying. Have the group fly the kites, the hosts and hostesses holding the kites of their guests. Desirable outcome: Satisfaction in providing pleasure for others.[1]

Even in a Progressive system, once in a while a teacher may be encountered who has a leaning toward teaching the fundamentals. It is not wise to muzzle such a teacher; therefore he is permitted to touch upon the fundamentals, but facetiously:

The teacher may tell a joke of what she heard—"Children, I heard a man in the street car this morning say 'It was me.' I knew you would like to hear the joke."

However, it is very dangerous to correct English too much, making the children too conscious of mistakes, because they are likely to embarrass their parents and elders at some inopportune time.[2]

In the eyes of Progressive education it is safer and therefore wiser to give the pupils training in things that cannot bring embarrassment to anyone. In Grade II:

Discuss the ways of making puppets—umbrella ribs or sticks with paper figures cut out and fastened on; clothespins or bottles dressed up; or rag dolls made of material.[3]

---

[1] St. Louis, op. cit.
[2] Los Angeles, op. cit.
[3] St. Louis, op. cit.

The pupils make a beanbag; convert a small box into a wagon; paint the above wagon with wagon paint.[1]

Note the admirable realistic touch here. Too much in the past the children have been permitted to "make believe," but Progressive education stipulates that the wagon constructed from a small box is to be painted with *wagon* paint—the real thing. The child, left to his own resources, might use ordinary stain or even water-colors. The children of this grade should show the ability to:

Recognize and name correctly papier-maché cheese boxes.
Recognize beauty in the most common things, as a bar of soap.
Recognize paper, cotton, wool, silk, jute, raffia by sense of touch with eyes closed.
Tell when an egg is not fresh.[2]

Apparently in training the pupils to tell when an egg is not fresh, the experts leave to the discretion of each teacher the decision as to whether or not the feat is to be performed with eyes open or closed.

It is important that a child come to have an attitude which will lead to acts of kindness, such as feeding a lost kitten—even sharing his milk with the friendless creature.[3]

At this level the child should reveal the ability to

[1] Los Angeles, op. cit.
[2] Los Angeles, op. cit.
[3] Los Angeles, op. cit.

raise caterpillars and tadpoles and to find them interesting. Also to

> Use handkerchief properly
> Bathe more than once a week
> Look for gladsome things.[1]

V

When the child gets to the third grade his creative impulses are to be directed along highly essential lines. He should learn to compound home-made ink and vegetable dyes and use these in making posters and dyeing cloth and yarns for weaving. He may borrow furnishings from the home and bring them to school so as to stimulate his efforts:

Simple articles used by the pupils in daily life, that can be easily procured and brought into the schoolroom, serve as models and relate to units of instruction such as food, clothing, travel, and occupation. Articles relating to clothing, as hats and caps, bags, suitcases, and coat hangers, are useful models. Sloyd tools and implements used in the home, as brooms, dusters, dustpans, coal buckets, and waste baskets, are excellent models. Even large articles can be brought to class to draw, as bicycle, wheelbarrow, cart, or doll buggy.[2]

Excursions into the outside world continue to play

---
[1] Los Angeles, op. cit.
[2] Los Angeles, op. cit.

an important part in the child's education, but now he is to be guided into avenues where the knowledge acquired is of a type which not only will interest him, but prove of lasting worth:

Go with the children on a street car to a bakery. Discuss the baker's part in helping society. Have the children meet the man who will explain the work. Desirable outcome: knowing an employee of the bakery. Allow the children to make bread with the dough prepared by the baker, if such dough is given to the children. Desirable outcome: An increased knowledge of how to mold and bake the bread. The children may receive a sample loaf of the bread from the guide. Desirable outcome: Pleasure in receiving the bread.[1]

At this level it is the teacher's privilege to put in a good stroke for perpetuating civilization by training the pupils to:

Look for the bright side of life.
Wash hands after visiting toilet.
Use and take proper care of handkerchief.[2]

By the time children reach the third and fourth grades they should be fairly proficient in collecting, cutting out, and mounting pictures, and it is now time to stress the subjects represented fully as much as the important techniques of using scissors and paste pot:

Almost any day one may find classes cutting and mount-

[1] St. Louis, op. cit.
[2] Los Angeles, op. cit.

ing pictures of things to eat, making price tags, separating the cards into groups such as breakfast, dinner, luncheon, or meats, fruits, vegetables, soups, breads, desserts. With these groups the classes play that they are choosing their meals. There is more interest and opportunity for practice if each article is mounted separately and if the children gather up the mounts containing pictures of food as the dishes containing the real food are collected in a cafeteria.[1]

Thus Progressive education, awake to its responsibility for the whole life of the child, undertakes to train pupils to wrestle with the big problems of intricate modern life. In earlier years many a child was turned loose on the world without even having been taught by the schools how to patronize a lunchroom where he could expect some aid from the waiters, but today the third-grade and fourth-grade pupils receive such training as will enable them to function even in an eating place where self-service prevails.

Hand in hand with this schooling in how to select dishes in a cafeteria should go guidance in the construction of beautiful and useful things. The teacher, however, is cautioned not to expect too much general appreciation for the products turned out under his supervision.

With the exception of stuffed dolls and cats made from discarded stockings and underwear, the simple toys that small children can make do not find much of a market.

[1] Los Angeles, op. cit.

If children enter into the selling business at all they must be taught to keep their standards high, and yet one must remember that little children's technical abilities are not those of the adult. A calendar in every way suitable to be sent as a gift to one's grandmother or other relative in the East, may have no possibilities as a salable article, owing to absence of interest in the maker. Decorations for outdoor sales tables or booths for home-cooked food, for the ever-present ice-cream cone and such things, offer a field for all the work these small hands can do; yet it is also a real work, and meets a real need.[1]

Since the toys and novelties produced during school time by pupils may not be readily marketed, Progressive education cleverly directs the pupils' efforts to the making of articles that can be given away. The teacher is to discuss the true meaning of Christmas—that is, the spirit of giving, with the expectation that the talk will suggest to the class:

Supplying a Christmas box for an institution where the residents are invalids, cripples of all ages, and homeless babies. Have the children construct such articles as:

Match scratchers	Waxed flowers
Decorated blotters	Painted clay vases
Penwipers	Kodak books
Picture frames	Books with good jokes pasted in

Desirable outcome: Recognition of the value of one's contribution to society. Spirit of cheerful giving. Interest in mankind.[2]

[1] Los Angeles, op. cit.
[2] St. Louis, op. cit.

How drab a creature appears the school child of years gone by when compared with the pupils nurtured by Progressive education! In former days Christmas was looked upon by youth as a time when others were to bring them gifts; now the child is led to assume the rôle of benefactor by presenting, say, to the crippled inmates of an old men's home, a decorated blotter, a penwiper, and a scrapbook of clipped jokes representing a child's idea of what is humorous.

Experience shows that once the child has been made to feel the satisfaction of devoting school time to such noble undertakings, his enthusiasm will carry him along indefinitely.

Early in the spring, the problem of supplying toys for hospital children was again discussed, and the group decided to make the Easter spirit as much like Christmas as possible, to make a large supply of gifts, to give away all they could, and to keep no Easter presents for themselves.

They worked every moment that could be spared and showed much ingenuity in collecting and using inexpensive materials. The result was that there were ready at Easter time thirty dolls—half of them dressed like Dutch boys and the rest to represent Easter rabbits; ten engines made out of tin cans and pasteboard boxes with button molds for wheels and all nicely painted; eight trains consisting of an engine and one car made from bogus paper and fastened to a piece of flooring three inches wide and eighteen inches long. . . .

On Friday morning before the Easter vacation, the toys were delivered to the County Hospital by two children chosen by the rest of the group. These two were allowed to visit the children's ward and they brought back interesting reports of what was said and done when the gifts were presented.

In the midst of the report, the door opened and in came three children from a neighboring third grade carrying big strawboard trays full of Easter favors for the fourth grade. The favors were cardboard dolls with heads made of all-day suckers and with dresses and caps of crepe paper—blue, pink, yellow, pale green, and lavender. And one child expressed the sentiment of the room when he said, "The Easter Bunny was good to us after all."[1]

VI

While the pupils in Grade IV are learning such essential arts as dyeing and painting designs on eggs for Easter, and are being taught "not to lose five and ten-cent pieces," they also should get training in vital social customs which a completely feminized educational system desires perpetuated. The boys are to be drilled in such rules for courtesy as:

> Boys take off hats or caps when speaking to ladies, holding them in hands during the entire time.
> Talk softly.
> When making some uncalled for noise, say "Excuse me."
> When leaving the room where others are sitting, you say "Excuse me."
> Boys and men should take off caps or hats in elevator.[2]

[1] Los Angeles, op. cit.
[2] Los Angeles, op. cit.

THE POOR ENRICHED CURRICULUM

In order that a fourth-grade pupil may know how nice a little gentleman he has become under the guidance of his female teacher, he is to be provided with a self-rating card which will enable him to score his own conduct on such points as:

Do I say "Pardon me" when I bump into anyone?
Do I look at my teacher when she speaks to the class?
Do I refuse to quarrel with my neighbor?
Do I wait until it is necessary before leaving my seat?[1]

Progressive education, striving to finish with its choice cultural veneer all children with whom it deals, undertakes to refine girl pupils who may come from homes where such vulgar practices as using perfumery are in vogue:

There was too much perfume in a fifth-grade room.
"Mary," said the teacher to one little girl, "Do you know where the perfume you use comes from?"
"From roses."
"Are you sure?"
Mary produced her bottle as evidence. She pointed to the picture of a rose and the label "White Rose." The teacher turned the bottle over and showed the name of the maker, one of the large meat-packing houses. That was a puzzle—did the packing company work with flowers as well as meat?
The teacher said they did not, that their perfumes are

[1] Los Angeles, op. cit.

made from some of the refuse of the packing house. Mary was shocked—her perfume discounted.

"Would you like to read the pamphlets I brought from Chicago last summer after visiting a packing house?" the teacher asked. "You may find out more about your perfume and tell the class what you discover. They may be surprised too."

Mary was pleased with this special attention. Her report was prepared under the teacher's guidance. There was a surprised class when Mary finished her talk, and the cherished perfumes were less popular.[1]

At this level the pupils are to be encouraged to draw and cut out streamers and sailboats; they learn to use a telephone; they discuss in class what a father has to know about arithmetic to keep his position. The affairs of the home can be made so much more enticing, to teachers as well as pupils, than problems which have no personal touch; consequently:

It is interesting and profitable for the child in Grades V and VI to know how much each article costs and how much money is spent on him. He probably does not have enough money to make it worth his time to keep an account of his own financial affairs, but the money which his father and mother spend for him will furnish enough items to make an account interesting.[2]

Home folks are sure to be keen about coöperating

---
[1] Los Angeles, op. cit.
[2] Los Angeles, op. cit.

with the schools in such attempts to provide classroom material which the child will consider worth his while. All parents should give precise information, for publishing in class, concerning what is paid for the children's hats, shoes, underwear, and even the cost for altering a father's old coat so that the son may wear it.

VII

When the boy advances to the sixth grade, he is to learn to be neat and clean because of individual and collective praise from the female teacher regarding his appearance. Just a touch of the erotic! His social training, however, is to be continued in such prosaic matters as:

Washing hands after visiting the toilet
Properly using and caring for handkerchief.[1]

The training in collecting pictures must persist, but interest is now to be centered on such subjects as automobiles and auto advertisements. These will lead to learned class discussions.

The children began comparing cars and their mechanism. They wrote for pamphlets about different cars. They talked about the merits and demerits of two-wheel and four-wheel brakes, mechanical and hydraulic brakes. They discussed air-cooled and water-cooled cars; steel bodies and wooden bodies; balloon tires and ordinary tires. So much interest was aroused in the different makes of cars that those inter-

[1] Los Angeles, op. cit.

ested in the same car formed a group. The class collected material about the various makes of cars, tried to find out what people want in a car, and the selling points of each group.[1]

Thus the sixth-grade pupil may be trained to sit in the family council when the question comes up of purchasing an automobile. He is schooled in all the selling points, and may save the family the bother of listening to various salesmen when they call and even propose to give a demonstration.

It is in this grade that the pupil's interest in physical education is to be stimulated by bringing to his attention such important considerations as:

Make scrapbooks of pictures of the right and wrong kind of clothing, shoes, etc., in regard to posture.

Guard against bodily harm through his increased ability and strength gained through participation in games, stunts, etc.

Avoid bodily harm by running, leaping, etc.[2]

The teacher should guard against the possibility that the pupils' cunning at constructing things, developed during the preceding years, may fall into disuse. Therefore the class is to be encouraged in such projects as making dolls and wagons for pupils in other classes:

The girls brought the goods. Most of the stuffing of the

[1] Los Angeles, op. cit.
[2] Los Angeles, op. cit.

dolls was done by the boys as their fingers were stronger and they could pack them well. They also sewed on the arms and legs; the girls sewed the seams on the sewing machine and dressed the dolls. The boys made their wagons at sloyd. They built them strong and then made them attractive by using bright-colored paints. All the work was done during school time.[1]

A truly promising citizen is this sixth-grade boy who, through games and stunts, is trained to avoid, say, being run down by an automobile, by leaping and jumping, and who can stuff rag dolls and sew on their arms and legs. He learns to care for and mend the garden hose and to make and apply tree whitewash. He is encouraged to bring caterpillars into the classroom, feed them, and watch their development into butterflies; bring his pets to class for study; have pet shows.

A friend of the school promised to lend to one room a chipmunk which she had caught and kept in captivity for several years. Before he was brought, the children set out learning how to care for him. After investigation for several days, they found out what chipmunks eat in the wild state. The teacher then told them what this one had been fed during his captivity. They were much interested to learn that he was very fond of candy, but that the amount given to him should be limited, as too much made him sick and even caused his hair to fall out. . . .

The first day the chipmunk spent in the schoolroom he

[1] Los Angeles, op. cit.

stayed in hiding. The children thought this strange, since he had been in captivity for some time; they thought he would be tame. Finally they realized that after all he was wild and would not come out among strangers until he was really hungry. The second day he came out to eat and gradually became less afraid. . . .

The chipmunk stayed with them for two weeks and grew very friendly. He would scamper about the room and go into their pockets after nuts. . . . Children came from other schools to see him and other rooms in this same school were invited to watch him.[1]

Here is an indication of the type of valuable information Progressive education thinks to impart whenever a class is so fortunate as to be able to borrow a chipmunk. Such significant training was not given to pupils in earlier years even though they continued through high school. It is desirable under democracy that every child should learn that too much candy will make a chipmunk's hair fall out. At some future day the pupil may have a chipmunk of his own and, should the pet start to get bald, the pupil might, in the absence of such schooling, resort to hair tonics or mange cures instead of cutting down the rations of sweets.

The pupil in the sixth grade is also to be initiated into big "worth-while" undertakings, such as a paper drive. The teacher is advised to have the class bring

[1] Los Angeles, op. cit.

papers and magazines to school to be sold for a worthy cause. The desirable outcome cited is: Less rubbish in the home. This should win all parents' endorsement of the project, since it is so much more sensible to cart rubbish of this kind to palatial school buildings, than to an ordinary city dump. Enthusiasm is to be stimulated in the advisory groups through having the pupils elect a paper booster who will use his ingenuity to stir up interest in paper collection.

One new school was sorely in need of a victrola. After much discussion the sixth-grade children decided to help buy one by inaugurating a paper drive. A committee was appointed to consult with the principal. They secured his permission to talk to the other classes. . . .

The results were almost overwhelming. The next week the pupils organized committees, collected and bound the papers, and made trips for papers to addresses handed in by other children. They gave committee reports from time to time and when necessary called on other children for help.

The disposition of the tons of paper collected was the next problem. The children called up the paper companies and reported the prices quoted for paper. One group visited a neighboring school to get the names of the paper companies to which they had sold and the price received. Trucksters were interviewed as to their charges for hauling the paper to the paper companies. Then the transactions were completed.

The children's paper drive was successful; the victrola is now in the school, and the next payment on it is guaranteed.[1]

This report on an activity indicates the useful training that can be given a sixth-grade pupil. He gets practical experience in buying on the installment plan. Moreover, if in later years the worst comes to pass and he is thrown out of work, he should be able to adjust himself readily in his reverses by taking up the vocation of collecting and selling old newspapers and magazines.

VIII

Having spent seven years of his life in this edifying educational environment, the lad is now ready to tackle the work of grades VII to IX, usually referred to as the junior high school. From the moment he enters this new division, the school atmosphere should be charged with greater dignity.

Arrange for an assembly program to be held the day after the New Sevens enter the Intermediate School. Speech by the principal or vice principal in which he discusses such problems as—the best type of lock to buy for one's locker.[2]

After locks have been purchased, the pupils in this group may be given training that will stand them in good stead should they in later years be called upon to serve as judges in a bathing beauty contest.

[1] Los Angeles, op. cit.
[2] St. Louis, op. cit.

Call upon each of the groups of the seventh grade to suggest the name of one of the girls to take the part of queen of the May Day Festival. From the number of names have the congress members select two candidates for queen and eight for the four maids of honor. This list of candidates should then be sent back to the groups, where the congress representatives will call for a vote to determine the groups' choice and report it back to the congress. In this way the queen and her four maids may be selected.[1]

Naturally, these activities do not consume all the time that can be set aside for socializing projects. The pupil should be afforded an opportunity to develop certain other abilities for which he doubtless will have use in adult life. He may be trained in the technique of conducting an excursion and, through the school paper, may gain experience in being interviewed for publication. His mind can be properly attuned for comfortable mingling with such patriotic groups as, say, the Ku Klux Klan.

Interest the pupils in the idea of adopting a name for their group. A name that has a genuine meaning to the pupils is worth a great deal. The use of a symbol appeals to their love of the romantic and mysterious. A name exerts a silent but powerful influence upon the highly impressionable adolescent. A few suggestions for group names: Roosevelt's Rough Riders, Topnotchers, Willing Workers, A. A. Group (American Always), and S. O. S. (Seeking of Success).

[1] St. Louis, op. cit.

Keep interest in the home-room team alive by asking for reports on games by the captains, allowing the groups to develop cheer leaders, write songs, and originate yells. Encourage the pupils to display originality in the use of slogans.[1]

Care must be taken that the students at this level do not get away from the play idea around which all earlier school work rotates, and so the teacher should plan with the class a program to study the harmful effects of overwork; lead them to see the need for play as well as for work. Desirable outcome: Knowledge of having a good time.

Unfortunately even under Progressive education youth falls into the practice of using naughty words: A feminized educational system suspects that the habit obtains only with the males.

Since the question of the use of clean speech is primarily a problem for boys, it should not be discussed in mixed groups. Have a member of the student council make a speech to explain the campaign for clean speech and the need for it. He can afford to be perfectly frank in his discussion with the boys, even going so far as to mention the objectionable expressions commonly used by them. Close by singing the school song or giving the school yell. It is well to remember that thrills are worth while, especially so in the period of early adolescence.[2]

[1] St. Louis, op. cit.
[2] St. Louis, op. cit.

THE POOR ENRICHED CURRICULUM

An effort can be made to train these youths for noble public-spirited citizenship. They are to:

Develop an attitude of disgust for lawbreakers.[1]
Report any child of school age who is not in school.
Report contagious diseases.
    However, they should discriminate between "snitching" to satisfy a grudge and informing the authorities for the general welfare.[2]

And as the youth completes so much public schooling as he may be required by law to take, the wonderful period can be brought to a close with a fitting celebration:

When the ninth grade is about to complete the course, appoint or elect a committee selected from among the IX-4 representatives to the grade congress to plan the program for the last assembly meeting of the class that is about to leave school. A jolly program given in the school building during school hours will provide the opportunity for a pleasant farewell. The party should be a jolly affair with games and dancing. Desirable outcome: Acquaintance with approved standards of dancing.[3]

IX

With this revelation of some of the really important things being done by Progressive education to enrich

---

[1] St. Louis, op. cit.
[2] Los Angeles, op. cit.
[3] St. Louis, op. cit.

the curriculum, it should not be difficult for the layman to understand why a lad, on starting to work, may discover that he lacks such training as the work-world demands, and be forced to take up the menial vocation of bundle boy. The scope of a student's schooling will, of course, depend in a measure upon the teachers to whom he goes for instruction. He may be assigned to teachers who wink at many of the ideas found in the course of study, in which case he will likely suffer through being drilled in the fundamentals. On the other hand, if his teachers all subscribe to the theory that a child should play his way through the grades, he may find himself in the happy state, at the end of his ninth grade, of knowing play and nothing else.

Apparently there is a conflict between Progressive education and business, due entirely to the stupidity of business. Commerce and industry have no license arbitrarily to set down certain fundamental subjects in which an eighth-grade, ninth-grade, or tenth-grade pupil should be proficient. Business should first consult the reigning educational theorists and ascertain what they, at the moment, regard as the proper training for a child. The prospective employer, being informed that Sam Jones has had ten years of school attendance, should not presume to test Sam's spelling, scrutinize his English, or quiz him on combinations of the multiplication tables. The Progressive school records its accomplishments with Sam in more essential abilities. It teaches him how to blow his nose and take care of his handkerchief; convert old underwear into rag cats; make and fly kites; dye Easter eggs; cut out sailboats; select dishes in a make-believe cafeteria; feed a chipmunk; dance according to approved standards; be interviewed for publication; see beauty in a cake of soap; produce home-made ink; give a school yell; avoid injury by jumping and leaping; select beauty queens; and even recognize jute with his eyes shut.

What if he cannot read, write, or decipher? A Progressive system may not be disposed to concern itself with such studies, lest they prove an obstacle in the way of showing the pupils a good time. Business would do well to consult the Progressives before formulating requirements for entrance into remunerative employment. Always there are theorists ready to convince the world of the rightness of the doctrines to which they, at any particular moment, subscribe. Invariably after the world has been convinced, something happens to show that the theories were a lot of bunk; but straightway these faddists find something new to substitute. That is apparent in the foregoing quotations from the courses of study of two large cities, where unquestionably there are many level-headed, earnest teachers still teaching the fundamentals.

In the dark ages of formal education, most of the time spent in school was devoted to subjects the mastery of which required effort on the part of the pupil; in addition, there was "home work." A prophet of Progressive education exposes the folly of this:

The child does not need to read or write in his business of growing up, and it is indeed wasteful to press him to learn these arts with great labor when a little later they can be mastered with ease and interest in much less time. . . . Home work is of doubtful value at any age. Even in high school and college the school day is sufficient for concentrated intellectual activity, leaving the evenings for social and other self-prompted occupations.[1]

X

By elimination so far as possible of such studies as call for direct effort or home work, Progressive education has released most, if not all, of the school day for activities which appeal to the child's love for play. The test for any proposed innovation is neither its possible utilitarian worth to the adult nor its conformity to hoary tradition. The test is rather its promise to afford the pupil pleasure. When account is taken of this, the type of curriculum being developed in Progressive systems readily justifies itself.

If the child's parents were civilized, they doubtless taught him to use the toilet long before he started to school; but it becomes great fun for child and teacher

[1] Marietta Johnson. *Youth in a World of Men.* New York; The John Day Co., 1929.

THE POOR ENRICHED CURRICULUM 117

to attack the matter from a new angle, possibly motivated with dramatics. Human beings, from infancy to second childhood, instinctively pause to gaze into shop-windows; but school is made tremendously appealing to the pupil if window gazing is treated as an educational project. In a truly Progressive system there should be no interruption to the serious work of the class, even though a chipmunk comes for a two-weeks' visit and spends its time prancing about among the pupils in quest of nuts, since there is not likely to be any serious work under way with which to interfere.

It might be presumed that, if Sam Jones had continued in school after the ninth grade, he would have learned some of the things he now studies, at great sacrifice, by attending night classes; but it is more likely that the time would have been devoted to his further socialization. He had not yet attained the age when the teacher could introduce such activities as making lather and soaping one's whiskers, or when the principal could speak in assembly on some such problem as the right kind of blade to buy for one's razor. He may have gained experience in selecting prize beauties, but not in wooing them. Such training might have come to him in the senior high school.

Balanced growth requires that all schools be coeducational. If John and Mary do not pay as much attention to geometry or history as they should because of their interest in one another, that becomes a problem for the teacher, but in no case should the attraction be scorned or inhibited. It should merely be controlled. Love is educational.[1]

Progressive education is the crowning glory of the American feminized public school. Its wonders could never have been accomplished by mere male teachers. They, like parents, are always too conservative. The parent has been afraid to experiment in the rearing of his offspring, and lacks the courage to take such hazards as the Progressive female educator is willing and anxious to chance when experimenting with other people's children. This explains why the Progressives are now building their program around the idea of the "whole" child, which calls for the school to supervise the life of the pupil for twenty-four hours of each day from nursery school to college.

Since with the enriched curriculum the Progressive school is taking over many things, some of which were formerly attempted in the home, and certain others "came" to the child just naturally, when its colossal program is put into operation generally, parents will have been relieved of all their traditional responsibilities for the rearing of their children. Will the home then retain none of its educational prerogatives? Perhaps. In instances where a parent does not wish his offspring to grow up illiterate, he may be permitted by the Progressive educationists to drill his children at home in the common-school subjects.

[1] Marietta Johnson, op. cit.

CHAPTER VI

PRUSSIANIZED PEDAGOGUES

The Teachers of Liberty

I

Whenever an American proclaims, as Americans are everlastingly proclaiming, that education is the bulwark of democracy, not a single voice in the din of patriotic amens is heard to propose an inquiry into the validity of the assertion. On analysis, this unanimity of assent is not surprising, but neither is it convincing. Relatively few of those who approve the declaration could formulate a sensible statement of the precise meaning to be conveyed by either *democracy* or *education*. Consequently, agreement is much simpler for them than an effort to establish the premises from which an argument, *pro* or *con,* would have to proceed.

But the reader is not to be bored—nor is the writer—with an attempt in this place to supply the missing premises. As to the meaning of *democracy,* we may appropriate Lord Bryce's dictum that it "means nothing more nor less than the rule of the whole people expressing their sovereign will by their votes." For the

Edmund Dulac

present purpose this ready-made definition will suffice. To it may be tagged the sequential deduction that certain types of education must needs prove the antithesis of a bulwark for democracy. For instance, any education which influences the people to repress their sovereign will rather than give it free expression could hardly be regarded as friendly to democracy. But education of just such promise is gaining favor among those who direct the public schools in the United States.

A moment's contemplation will carry any unprejudiced man to the conclusion that education, if it is to qualify as a defense for democracy, must be of a particular design. But without bothering about such contemplation, the American people have swallowed—hook, bait, and sinker—the thesis that *any* education, no matter what its character, will serve as a bulwark for democracy undefined. Their next step in credulity is to presume that the task of imparting this education may be delegated, with complete abandon, to the State, which, of course, is to function through the public schools.

The American pedagogue has accepted with alacrity this assignment on behalf of the schools; and for some years past the one theme which most frequently bobs up, whenever two or more of his craft are gathered in the name of public education, is the implied obligation of the schools to train citizens for democracy. In cases, doubtless, the willingness of educators to take on the contract has sprung from a virtuous sense of civic responsibility. But in other cases, and I suspect this means a majority, the response finds its urge in that weakness of many contemporary schoolmen for tackling anything new and easy, provided it furnishes an excuse for letting go of something old and difficult.

Educating citizens for democracy appears easy primarily because those who prate about the thing are pleased to see it enveloped in vagueness. To them the proposal, therefore, wears the irresistible allurement of an uncharted route; it opens up countless ways for superficial pedagogues to persuade themselves—and others—that they are getting somewhere when, in truth, they are merely riding at anchor.

II

While the several generations of Americans who are now headed toward senility were receiving their elementary schooling, it may have been intended that the educational system should impart the sort of education that would serve as a bulwark for a democracy conforming to Bryce's definition. If so, the success of the endeavor has not been signal. On the one hand, with each passing year the American people have been called upon to increase substantially the funds appropriated to schools for "making citizens"; on the other hand, each passing year has recorded a further decline in the percentage of the school's product which, by the most popular test of political functioning—voting—has qualified as active citizens. The consequence is that those who think of active private citizenship primarily as voting intimate that disaster threatens unless there is a change. Whether the troubles of American Democracy are due to nonvoting or some other cause, the fact remains that contemporary private citizens have not been so trained that they, to any appreciable extent, sense the existence of a real problem here, much less any need for them to attempt to solve it.

There is no intention of lodging upon the educational system full responsibility for this growing deflection of enfranchised citizens from the ballot box and widespread indifference to the things that may be done in the name of democracy; although, certainly, the schools must bear a substantial share of blame for whatever weaknesses appear in the functioning of American citizens today. The schools have taught, and still are teaching, the sort of insipid history and civics that tend to encourage neglect of all the political prerogatives and obligations belonging to the individual. In course of time they have shelved the idea that eternal vigilance is the price of liberty, and in its stead pupils are led to believe that if a private citizen respects the Eighteenth Amendment, memorizes the Constitution, and goes to church on Sunday, he may rest in smug confidence, presuming that the democracy planted long ago by the Fathers will continue to flourish under the benevolent care of machine-made statesmen.

It is futile to weep over spilled milk. No substantial improvement, perhaps, need be expected in those Americans who have already habituated themselves to neglecting their duties as citizens. It is difficult to teach an old dog new tricks, or to break him of old ones. But hope turns to the young-pup citizens who have yet to cast their first ballots; and there it is that public education beholds soft and pliable materials with which to experiment on a large scale. Consequently, school administrators are making elaborate programs —and budgets—for the training of democracy's future citizens.

It would be pleasant, of course, to presume that the public schools, having taken account of the defects in those citizens already turned out, can now be trusted to do a better job with this fresh material. But such a presumption would be unwarranted. What reason has the thoughtful layman for supposing that American school systems, so long as their present attitudes are unchanged, can or will impart the sort of education which, in truth, might serve as a bulwark for democracy, especially in view of the fact that public education, as administered in many American communities today, is easily the most arbitrary and undemocratic agency supported by public funds, and that in other sections schoolmen seemingly lack the wisdom and the courage to pry into the real problems of citizenship training?

III

In order to show wherein the public schools of today are incompetent to perform the task which they are thus so eager, apparently, to attempt, it is proper, first, to ascertain what demands a democracy makes on its schools. At this point, Nicholas Murray Butler, President of Columbia University, opportunely appears with the specifications:

It is for the educational system of a really free people so to train and discipline its children that their contribution to the national organization and national effectiveness will be voluntary and generous, not prescribed and forced.[1]

Here is democracy's order to its educational system. But turn to the public schools of countless American communities to ascertain if they seem capable of filling the requirements, and at once you will find that the very first demand that school administration there imposes on those asked to train and discipline democracy's future citizens is that the teacher himself shall make a severely prescribed and forced obeisance to whatever brand of political bunk, at the moment, is favored by the dominant politicians of that community.

[1] Nicholas Murray Butler, *The Meaning of Education.* New York; Charles Scribner's Sons, 1915.

Moreover, in most such communities it will be found that school patrons are less disposed to protest a circumscription of the teaching force by despotic administrators and state officials, than they are to encourage it.

In years past the most disastrous thing for an American educator to do was to stray from the path of moral rectitude. A teacher who acted contrary to the ethical standards established by New England Puritans, won summary dismissal and was subjected thereafter to persistent hounding. In order that the doors of all educational institutions should be closed forever against his further employment as a teacher, he was branded as indelibly as Hawthorne's Hester Prynne. There was something to be said in favor of education's austere attitude, since the pedagogue was expected to set his pupils a lofty example. Let us grant the justice of this position regarding the teacher and sex matters —it still obtains; but what is to be said of the fact that today in steadily increasing measure countless other rigid restrictions are being placed upon the pedagogue?

This public servant who is being delegated to train democracy's future citizens, in many instances is called upon to display, in his personal life, to snooping neighbors no less than to the student body, the sort of expressionless citizenship which, if ever it becomes general, would transform the American people into a tribe of spineless political puppets. In many an educational system, the teacher who shows a disposition, even in his life outside the school, to exercise any of those traits that are supposed to be the earmarks of a true democrat, thereby imperils his employment by that system and, perhaps, his professional career.

This growing tendency among school administrators and state officials to curtail the freedom of the teacher makes ineffectual any effort really to train citizens for democracy. It is proper, in passing, to acknowledge that certain educational units, for one reason or another, have resisted the temptation to circumscribe the teacher's freedom, while in other systems, at least up to the present, such interference with the freedom of the pedagogue has revealed itself only in mild form. Attention, however, is to be centered on school administration in communities where marked headway has been made in the matter of official interference with the personal freedom of the teacher. In these communities, the cornerstone of educational administration is a type of depotism that most likely found its way to America before the World War with a consignment of caviar.

What percentage such systems constitute of all educational units in the United States is problematical. But two rather significant points may here be noted. First, when the material in this chapter appeared as a magazine article, a schoolman from one of the more progressive states protested that the charges contained in it were too sweeping. He explained that a group of educators in his state had discussed the article among themselves and reached the conclusion that such situations as were pictured would not be found duplicated in more than fifty per cent of the units in their state. Bearing in mind that they were taking account of conditions in an educationally progressive commonwealth, and, even if we allow that their estimate may be correct, there remains the significant fact—my second point—that the tendency here discussed is a growing one, since not so long before the school officials in that state did not have sufficient authority to exercise it in building up an autocracy. Finally, whether such conditions as are here discussed obtain in fifty per cent, twenty-five per cent, or seventy-five per cent of American school systems, their existence, regardless of the measure, constitutes a big problem that must be considered by those who look to the public schools to train the sort of private citizens who will be able to carry on democracy.

IV

The schoolman is not entirely to blame for existing conditions. Perhaps, a preponderance of those today administering education in communities where the disposition is to circumscribe the freedom of the teacher, at some time or other in their own careers resolved to practice, in their administration, that form of democracy which ought to be universal in the field of American public education; but many of them soon discovered that where the superintendent, of his own election, was not inclined to be autocratic, civic bodies and patriotic societies, no less than machine politicians, stood ready to knock all affection for real democracy out of him. He felt called upon to make his administration despotic in order that he might impose on his subordinates such restrictions as these lay bodies and politicians thought should be imposed. The sad aspect, however, is that the schoolman complies with such demands from the outside not because he believes it will make the schools better, but his own job more secure.

This idea of the importance of the superintendent staying in office is being stressed in many communities to a point where the lay observer might naturally conclude that the first purpose of school administration there is not to create bulwarks for democracy, but to shield from any possible disturbance the man who occupies the superintendent's berth, which is a political rather than a professional conception of officeholding. Four or five years ago, a prominent educational journal published an editorial that bitterly arraigned a certain board of education because it had seen fit to dismiss its school superintendent. Without acquaintance with the local situation, the editorial assumed that the superintendent was dismissed for purely political reasons.

The writer of this editorial made an impassioned plea for strengthening the grip of all superintendents upon their jobs, and closed with the sublime proposal:

> Let there be legal provision whereby weak superintendents may be made strong and good ones be protected.

Thus an age which keenly senses the curse of overlegislation beholds an outstanding American school journal seeking to perpetuate by law the job-holding of weak superintendents, as if that should take precedence over the business of providing the best possible schools for children. Of course, there could be no legal provision whereby inherently weak superintendents would be made strong professionally; but, even without encouragement from educational journals, the professionally weak superintendent invariably seeks to make himself strong politically. He accomplishes this by forming alliances with those who most likely will be able to keep him in office, and his execution of their will is made the basis for his hope that they will protect him. Usually he succeeds so well that it becomes hazardous for subordinates in his own system not to uphold him.

In administering such a system, the authority of the superintendent, so far as his teachers are concerned, can readily be made that of a despot—and the tendency of such an administration naturally is toward despotism. The superintendent's commands must be obeyed as unquestioningly as the orders of an officer of troops in action—literally he is an officer in action, engaged in defending his tenure of office. Compliance with the commands he issues may require teachers to be unprofessional and downright dishonest. Since his retention in office has become an obsession with him, he insists that the performance of the schools shall be represented to the public always in a creditable light, even though untruthfully. This situation may be revealed in a concrete illustration.

V

Education has certified to the fact that there are marked inherent differences in the mental capacity of the individuals composing any unselected group. Some children go through school more slowly than others and, even then, may know less after having completed the journey. As a consequence, a child of a given age, who entered school as early as other children, may be in the third grade while most of the same chronological group are in the fifth. The third grader is written down as retarded.

No one should find fault with educational administration when it attempts to study this matter of retardation for the purpose of learning whether it is a perfectly natural condition or one which calls for remedial measures. But in late years superficial schoolmen have jumped at the conclusion that a large degree of retardation is a reflection on the schools. If it is a reflection, then, perhaps, the teaching should be improved. But the autocratic superintendent now being pictured decided that this reflection might be more easily eliminated by an arbitrary edict. Therefore, in his system, whenever retardation is disclosed in large volume, the order is that pupils' marks are to be pushed up to the passing grade regardless of the quality of the school work done, or else, even where a pupil fails in one, two, or three subjects, he is still to be promoted in all subjects.

In a school system where there may be three, six, or ten thousand teachers, not one will be found with sufficient courage to refuse to follow such arbitrary instructions, although compliance must represent a crime against both the child and those who pay the bills for public education. But superintendents who can issue such unbelievably autocratic orders and know they will be obeyed, and servile instructors who receive these commands and observe them, in combination represent the sorry agency which in many communities it is proposed shall be entrusted with the designing and construction of bulwarks for democracy.

With the rapid expansion of the administrative phase of public education, the autocratic superintendent invariably appoints to the positions of assistant superintendents, supervisors, and experts, those employees who are sympathetic toward his practices and who show themselves most willing to serve the superintendent's personal ends. In the typical public school system of this class, they fare best who serve the superintendent best, and the standard for promotion becomes subservience to the chief. As usually happens in such cases, the obsequious subordinate, promoted because he subscribes to the sort of loyalty which prompts him, when his master slaps his one cheek, to turn the other for cuffing also, quickly learns to ape his master when dealing with those who now fall under his authority. Consequently, the superintendent's aides become a clique bent upon furthering the master's absolution.

An ambitious young man was lately given probational appointment as a principal of a night school in a large American city. Taking his cue from the superintendent's assistants, it became his first aim to make such a showing for the institution, on paper, that it would appear to reflect credit on the superintendent—and himself. He impressed members of the teaching staff with the necessity of pushing attendance up. If it fell off, he warned, some of the instructors might lose their positions, since night school appointments were conditioned upon sufficient pupils appearing for a subject to make up a class.

This principal succeeded in setting a new record for attendance, but apparently neglected to enlist the coöperation of the ruler of the universe. Unexpectedly, there came a week of heavy snow, strong wind, blizzards, and interrupted street-railway service. Attendance met a fate similar to that of Humpty-Dumpty. But this ambitious principal readily disposed of all evidence of the celestial interference, just as autocratic administrators had taught him to dispose of the presence of retardation. He ordered his teachers to disregard actual attendance and to mark down such figures as would indicate no falling off during the stormy period. The teachers, as most pedagogues under despotic administration would, obeyed, although several indiscreetly complained on the outside against the humiliation of being required to fake their records.

A busy-body heard of the affair and started an investigation. The teachers were willing to confirm, in confidence, the rumors that had reached this layman, but not one would consent to have his name used. The investigator then interviewed most of the students who had been present during the stormy week, and from them obtained information that enabled him to work out an approximation of the actual attendance. With these data in hand, he sought permission from the administrative officials to inspect the attendance records of the school. This request aroused some suspicion, and he was asked to explain his purpose. He made a frank explanation, and again demanded the privilege of inspecting the records. After being required to wait several hours, he was informed that the records wanted could not be located, although they should have been filed at least a month previously. He was invited to return later.

On the occasion of his subsequent appearance, he was handed a freshly typewritten statement of the attendance. This statement was not on the printed form used in the system; the figures did not represent those which, at the command of the principal, had been turned in by the teachers. But the investigation accomplished at least one noteworthy end. It revealed to the superintendent the sort of things this ambitious young man was capable of doing. Shortly thereafter he was made an assistant superintendent.

VI

Turning from the school administrator to the classroom instructor in a thoroughly autocratized system, and it need occasion no surprise to find that the teacher is denied anything which, with the widest stretch of imagination, could be regarded as professional or personal freedom. He does not dare speak out regarding school matters if his words can be construed as questioning the efficiency and professionalism of the administrative office. Even when subjected to most unfair treatment by his immediate superior, he may complain, if at all, only to that offending superior. He must take his choice between being a rubber stamp of approval for everything his superiors do or else suffer such discrimination against himself as will make life miserable. No matter how superior his professional training, he must meekly adopt the methods and practices which supervisors, who may have gained their positions through bootlicking chiefly, may impose on him.

He casts his professional career to the winds if he is guilty of practicing, even when outside the schools, the sort of democracy in which he must perforce pretend to believe in order to hold his job. In such systems, the signs of *verboten,* which for the educator once fenced off only the field of venery, today literally hem him in on all sides from everything that even remotely suggests freedom. In matters of education, science, religion, economics, government—his thoughts, speech, action are all prescribed for him by his superiors.

Attention may first be directed toward the teacher as a technically trained individual who should be encouraged to make a voluntary and generous contribution to the nation's stock of knowledge on school matters. If the average teacher in such systems as are now being considered has any opinions of his own on professional subjects, he must conceal the fact as closely as if those opinions were a loathsome disease. Even when we turn to those communities where education may have escaped the hand of depotism, we find that the pedagogue is offered little encouragement to seek emancipation, but on every hand educational leaders appear ready to affirm that no teacher can justify himself for discussing school matters if his comments can be interpreted in such fashion as to appear to criticize practices and conditions in the school system with which he finds employment. No matter how iniquitous a situation may become, he is to feel that his loyalty commands him to keep his mouth shut so long as he stays in that system. Should he feel that he simply must speak, then the only honorable course for him, he is told, is to resign before he utters his first word of criticism, and then to speak as an outsider.

A typical instance is that of a Wisconsin teacher who, after more than a quarter century of distinguished service, was summarily dismissed because "in the opinion of the Superintendent and Board of Education she was guilty of unprofessional conduct." She ran counter to a principle "that every school organization must recognize, namely, that there is an obligation upon every individual who works in the group to support the policies of the organization." About the only important policy this teacher opposed was the act of her superintendent in having a course of study constructed, at a cost of more than six thousand dollars of public money, ostensibly for the schools, but actually to produce the basis for a dissertation which the superintendent wished to offer for a doctorate to be conferred upon himself. Subsequently, happily, certain citizens of the community raised a fund to carry the case to court and the outcome was that the teacher was reinstated, although her health had been seriously impaired through the experience. The superintendent was dismissed.

VII

Not long ago the superintendent of a large city system was confronted with an educational problem which he sought to solve by political methods. The teaching staff was underpaid; various civic groups had become aroused and were demanding better salaries for the teachers. But the politicians in control of the municipal government intimated that they would not favor a budget which might threaten to increase the tax rate, lest this operate against them in the next election. The superintendent decided to straddle the situation, and proposed a nominal increase in teachers' salaries, but at the same time ordered a marked increase in the size of elementary classes, so that the actual number of teachers employed could be reduced. When the scheme became known, the local press, realizing that this superintendent knew little about elementary education, invited certain people who were generally regarded as authorities to express an opinion concerning the plan. Among those interviewed was an elementary principal who had been in the system several decades and who had been honored with high office by various professional groups.

This teacher discussed the effect of the size of the class upon classroom instruction. She pointed out that when a class was expanded beyond a certain point, the effectiveness of the teaching took a disproportionate drop. She expressed the belief that the average elementary class in that city was then at the maximum size for proper handling. This teacher could have quoted countless educational authorities for everything she said. But for daring to express an opinion that could be construed as not endorsing unconditionally a foolish makeshift proposed by the superintendent, she was slated for punishment. Although she was an exceptionally good teacher and at the height of her efficiency, an order was issued that she immediately apply for retirement, thereafter to subsist on a miserable pension representing deductions made from her salary in previous years; otherwise she would be "tried and fired." Moreover, a school board composed of supposedly representative citizens promptly thereafter passed a resolution which made it insubordination for any teacher in the system to express his views on educational matters except in private to the superintendent.

According to those codes of ethics for teachers that have been graciously prepared for them by superintendents and college professors of education, this teacher, seeing the school system imperiled by a false economy measure, should have resigned before presuming to air her views, or else she should have remained silent and become an accessory to a crime both before and after the act. Supposing she had had a strong martyr complex and had stepped into private life, what would have been her status as a constructive critic? At a nod from the superintendent, the entire "loyal" teaching force of that city would have been ready to discredit her by passing resolutions, prepared perhaps by the superintendent himself, upholding his noble administration against the attacks of disgruntled former employees of the system.

VIII

Enough has been said to show that, in our autocratic systems, if the teacher attempts professionally to be a democrat, he books himself for destruction. It is not necessary here to go into details concerning his prescribed and forced attitude on matters of science. Certainly the reader is acquainted with the movements in various parts of the country to prohibit teachers from so much as mentioning the theory of evolution. Finally, the instant an educator begins to discuss the political administration of his community critically or government comparatively, he bares his head for a crown of thorns. Here we have a situation that surely obtains much more generally than some of the other forms of the teacher's circumscription. To an amazingly large degree the American teacher does not dare, even in his out-of-school life, to inquire into the operations of government critically or to discuss current political theories and practices candidly without bringing down upon his head censure, if not from his immediate superiors, then from other state officials and patriotic organizations.

How, then, is this restricted individual to train the young of the country to be more efficient citizens than their forebears, since the first step in such training, perhaps, should be an endeavor to make future citizens assume a more inquisitive and critical attitude toward the social and industrial orders as well as toward political administration?

A magazine which is by no means radical offered a series of small prizes for original definitions of socialism. On the whole, this contest was a commendable one, since, especially in the United States, so much is said about socialism by those who, in ignorance, suppose that a socialist is merely an anarchist by another name. Henry Flury, a teacher of biology in a Washington (D. C.) high school, won the sum of $5.00 with a perfectly harmless composition of about two hundred words. Shortly after its publication, some snooper made the startling discovery that a public school teacher of the national capital had dared to define socialism; whereupon, one Major General Amos A. Fries went into action with a demand that the Washington school system be purged of the "dangerous" man.

Rather than attempt an interpretation of the army officer's mode of attack, excerpts may be presented from the original documents in the case so that the reader may draw his own conclusions. The first broadside by the Major General, a letter addressed to the Superintendent of Schools, set forth:

The American Legion stands for God and country. It stands for a vigorous Americanism. It stands for nationalism and the vigorous upholding of the Constitution of the United States. It is for that reason that as Commander of the American Legion for the Department of the District of Columbia, I object most strenuously to the ideas put forth in *The Forum* by Mr. Flury and against anyone being kept in the schools of the District of Columbia who says in effect that workmen in America are slaves; that our civilization is cruel; that little children still toil in factories (some do but very few and lessening all the time); who says that those who toil in building automobiles, Pullmans, and palaces, walk and live in boxcars or in hovels. Anyone who has gone to the factories of Henry Ford, or who has taken the trouble to go where building operations are in progress anywhere in this city, will find that the majority of the workmen ride to their work in their own automobiles. He will probably find also that they get paid equally well or better than high-school teachers.

Finally, in asking the question, "Is not the Industrial Civilization we have created a Frankenstein that has made itself our master?" he is using only a slightly different form of the statements of the communist that our form of government is bad. The communist then adds that our government should be overthrown and if necessary by force and violence. This is just the type of un-American radicalism that the American Legion and other patriotic organizations are bitterly opposed to. Particularly are they bitterly opposed to this sort of stuff being taught to our boys and girls. . . .

I am writing you this letter at once to find out . . . what action you propose to take in the matter. I shall await your answer before taking the matter up with the various patriotic organizations in this city.

Such a communication addressed to the average superintendent might have brought prompt dismissal of the "offending" teacher, regardless of any injustice attendant on the course. Doctor Frank W. Ballou, the schoolman to whom the letter was addressed, was not so easily awed. He acknowledged the letter by promising to read the article in question and also ascertaining whether Mr. Flury had been guilty of presenting unpatriotic views to his students. To this the Major General replied:

As far as reading the article is concerned, the paragraph that I sent you was all there was to it. However, it is simply using the questionnaire form to put forward certain ideas which, in a different form, would be put forth as opinions. There has not been any question raised as to whether or not Mr. Flury has done this in the schools. The point which I am decidedly interested in is whether he is the author. A man who will write such a definition of socialism has, in my opinion, a mind so constituted and ideas so warped as to be unsafe. I shall be delighted to hear from you in regard to this man.

Doctor Ballou made an investigation and reported on this to his School Board. The Board then wrote the Major General:

From the evidence before the Board it appears that the article to which you refer was written by the teacher in a competition inaugurated by the magazine in which it appeared. The facts are that the teacher is a teacher of science. He entered the United States Army as a volunteer and received an honorable discharge under date of December 9, 1918. The views or beliefs expressed in the article referred to have found no place in his classroom teaching, in his discussions or conversations with the faculty or with the patrons of the school. The Board of Education believes that every individual is entitled to entertain his or her own private views regarding religion, the functions of Government, and political and economical issues without necessarily involving questions of loyalty with respect to the fundamental ideals of our institution.

The type of man who would be fit to serve a democratic government, even as an attaché of the army, should take great pride in the position assumed by this particular board of education, just as he should be disinclined to acknowledge authorship of the two communications signed by the Major General. Let us note, however, the effect of the Board's conclusions upon the accuser:

Major General Amos A. Fries, chief of the Army Chemical Warfare Service, does not intend to drop his efforts to get Henry Flury, Washington high school teacher, discharged from his post for writing a definition of socialism, he said in an interview today. Both as a taxpayer with children in the local schools—although not in the school where Flury teaches—and as commander of the American Legion for the District of Columbia, Fries asserts he intends to push his demand for Flury's dismissal, despite the refusal of the Board of Education to act.

Anyone who wants to "cast aspersions on our country" is un-American and should not be permitted to teach school, no matter whether he keeps his private views out of the classroom or not, Fries said. . . .

When it was pointed out that Flury's definition said nothing about overthrowing the present civilization or government, as Fries' letter had charged, Fries replied that "the insinuation is still there. In a different form he is advancing the same ideas you find in the rankest communistic papers and magazines." He said his objection was to Flury's apparent "finding fault with our civilization. It is the best the world has known."[1]

IX

Bearing in mind how, not so many years before, spokesmen for the Federal Government sought, through condemnation of Germany's dominant militaristic spirit, to rouse to fighting humor meek American citizens who had been drafted for a war in defense of democracy, it is interesting to note how, now

[1] *Evening Sun*, Baltimore, Nov. 18, 1926.

that the world has been made safe for democracy, representatives of the military department of the Government seek to do a bit of Prussianizing on their own account. Although the champions of militarism have not yet succeeded in cowing the school officials of Washington, where the superintendent happens to be a courageous pedagogue, in other cities their efforts have been crowned with success.

A group of instructors and students at the West Chester (Pa.) Normal School met from time to time to discuss current problems. They called themselves the Liberal Club. On one occasion the members engaged in a discussion of the course of the Federal Government in Nicaragua—a matter that was being debated in Congress and throughout the country. Officials of the American Legion straightway charged the Club's members with "creating disrespect to the President and the Government by questioning their Nicaraguan policy." Andrew Thomas Smith, principal of the school, while acknowledging that he had "personally defended the Liberal Club, whose attitude and purpose are not now under consideration," commanded the Club to cease to function because it had displeased some factotum of the American Legion. Doctor Smith is reported to have said:

Whoever goes into print following this demand goes in at his own peril. If you disregard this advice, don't complain if some one knocks you on the head; it may hit you many ways. . . . I understand perfectly the spirit of the mob.[1]

Perhaps the Liberal Club was seeking to keep alive a remnant of the "Spirit of '76." At all events, it pursued its course regardless of the displeasure of the Legion's mouthpiece and the command of the cowed principal. The consequence was that two members of the faculty—Professors Robert Kerlin and John A. Kinneman—were "hit on the head" by the Board of Trustees, which in summarily dismissing the men advertised to the world that the spirit of the mob is not always found only with the mob. Major John A. Farrell, of the Legion, sealed the incident with the beautiful dictum:

There is no justification for students in a tax-supported institution to criticize the government that gives them an education.[2]

Go a step further North, and you find that the Board of Education of New York City has asserted that a teacher whose political views are not pleasing to his superiors may be denied a square deal on that account. Among the notable recent additions to the vast literature dealing with bills of rights, this New York City contribution takes ranks on the low level:

In determining whether or not a teacher shall be promoted, the Board of Superintendents is obligated to take

[1] *Sun*, Baltimore, Apr. 12, 1927.
[2] *The Nation*, Apr. 6, 1927.

into account the history of the teacher, his public opinions, the persons with whom he associates, and his attitude toward governmental questions. A teacher may not have one set of opinions for the classroom and another for the public platform. As a schoolteacher, he has not the same rights as other citizens to print, publish, or declare his thoughts and opinions. He is no longer at liberty to "freely write, speak, or publish." This is not an interference with his rights as a citizen. His rights are as "free and untrammeled as they ever were." He may at any time emancipate himself from the shackles of the department and exercise his full rights as an American citizen by resigning his position.

It is almost unbelievable that such an undemocratic statement should have issued officially from the largest public school system in this country. But there it is. It says in effect that anyone who would train citizens for democracy must consent to assume the rôle of a serf; to be muzzled; to wear shackles. If officials see fit, where educational administration has become corrupt, to cheat democracy even to the extent of not giving the child a decent common school education, this enslaved pedagogue must help in the cheating. When it comes to the matter of training children so that they will assume a wisely critical attitude toward their agent—the government—the enslaved teacher is not to open his mouth except for the purpose of drilling additional voices for the idiotic chorus—"My Country, right or wrong!" Yet this pedagogue does not dare by his action to show that he really believes it is *his* country and that he constitutes a unit in the sovereign will of the whole people. When the disposition is to penalize a teacher for speaking critically of government, there naturally is offered a temptation to commend political administration dishonestly in the hope of being rewarded. Thus the real incentive becomes to praise government rather than try to improve it, and under such false commendation government is encouraged to deteriorate further.

Public education, under its present trend in many sections of the country, sets up an example of citizenship in the life of the teacher that constitutes a greater insult to American democratic institutions than all the mouthings of the Reds and the near-Reds. Where this thing of undemocratizing the public schools may end, is not easy to forecast; but already the job has progressed so far that it would hardly be amiss if we began flying the American flag, upside down, on many an American schoolhouse.

CHAPTER VII

PUBLIC EDUCATION FEMINIZED

Fallacy of Equal Salary Scales

I

One of the few issues which American Democracy seems to have settled with finality is that government should not discriminate between the sexes in the matter of salaries paid school teachers. Surveying this settlement superficially, the layman may conclude that he is not interested in the subject. He is prone to remain placid even though warned that an equal salary scale may eventually lead to a feminizing of the entire educational system, including the state institutions of higher learning. Perhaps he would become aroused if persuaded that the extent to which feminization has already progressed imposes an educational handicap upon his own child, and, accordingly, might be moved to attack the problem. But what chance would there be of having the decision reversed? Certainly not a fat one!

More and more the adjustment of teachers' salaries is coming to rest in the hands of those on the payrolls of the schools—persons who, to put it mildly, are likely

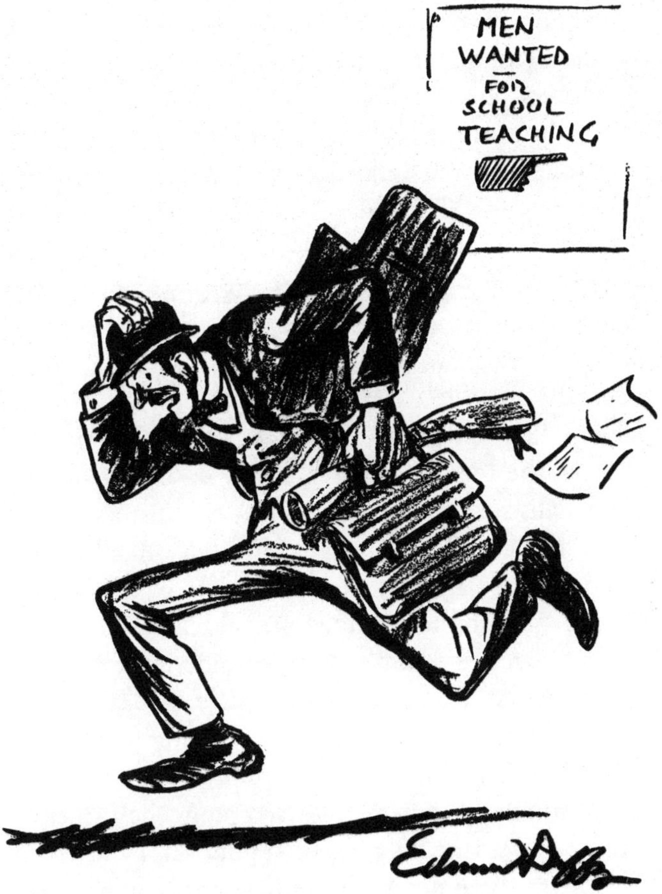
MEN
WANTED
FOR
SCHOOL
TEACHING

to be prejudiced always in their own favor. This group, the teaching and supervising force, as now constituted, is overwhelmingly female—so much so that even careful writers on educational matters invariably use the term *school teacher* as of feminine gender. Put these facts together—the influence teachers *en masse* exert in determining their salary scale with the supremacy of the female sex in the force—and the inescapable conclusion is that when this rate-fixing power of uneven sexly complexion essays to construct a schedule, it is not likely to show partiality toward its minority element, the male teachers. Though the crying need of public education today may be more and better male teachers, the female majority, urged on by the aggressive equalists in their midst, will surely turn a deaf ear to the cry, should heeding it threaten an advantage already gained by them in the matter of being paid salaries equal to those offered men teachers.

It is altogether sensible when considering the merits and demerits of an equal salary scale to bear this in mind. The female element of the teaching force under aggressive leadership has been strong enough to coerce most educational systems into accepting the principle, and, wherever the thing has been put over, by that very process the position of the female element has been further strengthened. Moreover, the female pedagogue when she undertakes to fight for monetary recognition, is more militant than our lamented sister, the late

Carrie Nation. Mrs. Nation had to do her stuff alone and with no more formidable a weapon than a department-store hatchet, whereas female teachers have cleverly marshaled powerful and snappy forces for support. Parent-teacher associations in the smaller political divisions; teachers organizations in counties and states; national and international societies for unifying feminine effort—these are prepared at all times to wage war unrelentingly not only for higher salaries for women teachers, but against any differentiation in pay based on the sex of the teacher.

II

In analyzing the chief point made in favor of an equal salary scale, a modified form of the case study method—a popular one with educators—may be employed. First, there is the instance of Miss X, a comely, up-to-the-minute girl who thinks to go into teaching because it is a noble profession for women—it pays well. Next, there is the case of Mr. Y, a young fellow who has a leaning toward pedagogics but wants to make sure that teaching will afford him a decent living.

Both of these subjects, measured by all the gauges devised for determining the possibilities of converting student material into classroom teachers, are found to possess the same qualifications—intelligence, personality, interest, ambition, and character. Both will be expected to follow identical courses of professional training, and, when they take up their work, it is supposed that each will deliver the same quality and quantity of service. Under democracy, whose slogan is equality, what right, then, has the State to ask Miss X to work for a lower salary than Mr. Y, or, to put the thing in the form it more frequently assumes, to propose a higher salary for the man teacher? From Maine to California the answer, soprano, rolls in: *None!* Therefore, the matter is settled for all time, and the female who goes into teaching expects to receive exactly as much money as is paid a male teacher for the same work.

The decision seems patriotic; it appears to conform to the spirit of the nineteenth amendment—a constitutional proviso which is respected in the same measure that the immediately preceding addition to our organic law is scorned; it is also courteous to those ladies who are likely to forget their proverbial attribute of gentleness and become belligerent if anybody questions the rightness of the decision. Let a politician propose that the State discriminate against female teachers because of their sex, and a mighty army of Amazons, replacing the lipstick with warpaint, will be mobilized by the feminine equalists and put upon his trail. Life certainly would be made miserable for any public official who at this day should openly suggest a differentiated salary scale as a democratic measure.

The most significant phase of the matter is that the arguments which led American Democracy to settle upon an equal salary scale are based upon false premises. If we believe in democracy, then we are bound to hold that in the matter of public education the same work should bring the same remuneration regardless of the sex of the worker, provided only, of course, that we are willing to subscribe to the principle that the public schools under democracy are maintained for the benefit of the teacher. Few teachers will allow such intimation to go unchallenged; they will proclaim, with great gusto, that the chief concern of the public school is neither parent nor teacher, politician nor school janitor, but the student body, and that the sole justification for a state-financed educational system is the child.

But the child has not been seriously considered by those who have labored for an equal salary scale. Most discussions of teachers' salaries by contemporary female pedagogues are weighted down with platitudinous references to the child, his interests, his needs, his rights, and society's responsibility in seeing that he gets a fair start in life. Strip these discussions of mere verbiage, and all that remains of the child, as a rule, is a cat's paw to be used by educational opportunists to draw more money from the public exchequer. In much the manner that dyed-in-the-blood villains in popular fiction of an earlier age starved and even mutilated little children in order to convert them into effective beggars, so today, in a less vicious manner, to be sure, but just as daringly, the child is too often paraded before the public, his simple needs made direful, primarily with a view to having him procure something that will benefit his teachers but which may actually injure him. For a brief space, let us cease confusing the pedagogue's interests with the actual needs of the pupil, and look at the matter of teachers' salaries with regard solely for the good of the child.

III

The enormous and steadily increasing sums being spent upon public education annually are not justified except it can be shown that the schools are accomplishing the ostensible purpose for which they exist—taking the youth of the land and training them to become useful and efficient citizens. Admission that youth are not being trained adequately in this respect is found in the fact that educators at present devote meeting after meeting to a discussion of shortcomings in current endeavors at citizenship training. How far responsibility for this failure rests upon an overfeminization of public education would make an interesting study, if any schoolman had the courage to undertake it, but none would even dare propose attacking the problem from this angle, despite the fact that it is so apparent that pupils, both male and female, are not

PUBLIC EDUCATION FEMINIZED 157

now getting a properly balanced tutorial diet. After all, the revolt of youth of both sexes is a natural and expected reaction of the child who has become satiated with exclusively feminine educational environment. Leading educational authorities have testified to the importance of providing competent men teachers for pupils above the lower grades. Thorndike[1] years ago admitted that "it would almost certainly be a gain for the teachers of boys and girls to include a larger proportion of men if the best men would do that work with equal zeal." Briggs,[2] noting the complaint that "in early adolescence pupils do not get the needed influence of teachers of both sexes," said: "There is no implication that men are better teachers than women; the assumption is that there is a need for the example and influence of both men and women on boys and girls who are tending to set their ideals and attitudes toward many matters of life." Snedden,[3] then Commissioner of Education for Massachusetts, declared that "a certain proportion of men teachers should be assigned to departmental positions, not primarily because they are necessarily better teachers than women, but because it is desirable to introduce, in boys' classes at

[1] Edward L. Thorndike. *Education: A First Book*. New York: The Macmillan Co., 1912.
[2] Thomas H. Briggs, *The Junior High School*. Boston: Houghton Mifflin Co., 1920.
[3] David Snedden. "Reorganization of Education for Children from 12 to 14 years of Age." Baltimore: *Educational Administration and Supervision*, September, 1916.

any rate, the influence of masculine personality." Further testimony is found in the great ado which schoolmen make today when they can report even a meagre sprinkling of males among the students enrolled in teacher-training institutions.

But in the face of such admissions as to the desirability of getting men into the teaching profession, the records show that school administrators have permitted the percentage of male teachers in the public schools to drop from 42.8 per cent in 1880 to 17 per cent in 1926, and the decline is going on merrily. Men have been eliminated almost entirely from the elementary grades; they have only a flimsy representation in the junior high school; the day seems not far distant when they will disappear from the senior high school; and then will follow their extinction as instructors in state-supported institutions of higher learning, where the invasion of women teachers is going on at a rapid pace.

We find the youth of the land—boys and girls—subjected in most instances to tutoring exclusively by women during the entire period spent in the elementary grades and to an enormous and rapidly increasing extent during the years spent in high schools. Thorndike[1] as early as 1912 asserted that "something like half of the boys and girls in city schools never have a man as teacher." He noted that "One may

[1] Op. cit.

regret the fact . . . and yet not regret their not having the particular men who could be got, at the same salaries, to replace the women now teaching the upper grammar grades."

IV

Admit, frankly, that the teaching profession today is attracting high-grade women, and we must allow, in the next breath, that for actual teaching positions decidedly inferior males are being recruited. It is a matter of common kowledge that, where the student body is exposed to male teaching, especially in the elementary grades and the junior high school, the male pedagogue to whom he goes for instruction does not usually represent a high-grade animal, so that, where a child gets a mixed instructional diet, it is of uneven quality with the men teachers markedly inferior to the women. Indeed, a blanket charge might be made against male teachers in this group, of offering justification for a feminizing of the school system. Certainly as much is intimated by Thorndike in the passage quoted.

We find, then, that while young people, certainly from the age of twelve on, should be provided with both male and female teachers, the pupil either is denied an opportunity to profit by male instruction or else he must elect a decidedly weak male teacher over a relatively strong female teacher. An educational institution where, from the seventh grade up, the faculty is composed of a sexly mixture of high quality, will afford a much better atmosphere for the mental and moral growth of the child than can possibly exist at an institution staffed entirely with women. But not only will the child benefit under such a mixed faculty, the individual members of the staff will also be benefited. With no wish to disturb the self-sufficiency of the women, we must assert that they will improve as instructional agents if, in their daily professional work, they are brought into contact with male teachers who are their peers, just as they deteriorate surely when they are forced into contact with decidedly inferior men on the teaching staff.

If a representation of high-grade males on the faculty will result in direct benefit to the child because of his contact with such instructors, and also in an indirect way through the improvement of the faculty in its entirety because of the presence of male instructors, then, for the sake of the child, democracy should place in the elementary schools as well as in the high schools a substantial percentage of male teachers.

The pupil, coached by those who know the sort of instructors he requires, comes before the American people and insists that, if he is to be developed in such manner as to justify the expenditures being made on public education, it is essential that he be freed from female pedagogical dominance and be permitted to react to the teaching, as well as the classroom influence, of a mixed faculty of uniform quality. Supposing, thereupon, the American people should instruct school administrators to go out and hire the type and assortment of teachers the child requires—what would they find?

At a certain figure, let us arbitrarily say $2050.00 a year, they can hire a fairly creditable woman elementary teacher—Miss X. At the same figure, on an equal salary scale, they cannot entice Mr. Y to enter the teaching profession. This is a hard-boiled fact that cannot be softened with sentiment or even female tears; moreover, the same situation will confront school administrators for many generations to come, if not always. Whether in the mind of Miss X, a male teacher such as Mr. Y is worth only the same salary as can be offered her need not be considered. The single vital point is that this child requires the services of Mr. Y; but Mr. Y declines to give his services at the same price that is offered Miss X. School administrators may, foolishly, presume that if they push the salary up a bit, they will land Mr. Y; not realizing, apparently, that the disturbing feature to Mr. Y is not a matter of dollars and cents, but of equal salary. An analysis of the situation will show that Mr. Y's demand for a premium because of his sex is not nearly so arbitrary as might at first appear.

V

Miss X, receiving $2050.00 a year, can support herself adequately. For those who demand it, a bit of sentiment may be sprinkled over her case—it will blow off promptly. Allow that Miss X makes herself responsible, in part at least, for the maintenance of a home. She has a mother who is unable to earn; a father who is unwilling to earn; or a brother who is too stupid to earn. Because of this domestic situation, she may be called upon to use a considerable part of her salary in supporting others. But sentiment ceases to function when account is taken of the probability that the home she helps to maintain, when once she begins to draw her $2050.00, can be made a better one because of this contribution than the home in which she was reared. In short, her professional career enables her to raise her own standard of living.

Again, she may marry, since celibacy is no longer required of women teachers. However, if she thinks to continue in the profession, she doubtless will find it desirable to avoid motherhood; therefore marriage will not add to her financial burdens unless she ventures foolishly. If the consort she elects is worth a huckle, he will bring home his share of the bacon; if he is just a bum—and occasionally a fairly high-grade woman teacher goes slumming for her romance—she can, by diverting her customary alms, keep this acquired encumbrance in a state befitting a bum.

Mr. Y, on the other hand, when he casts about for a vocation, will refuse to be attracted to a calling that will not provide the means for setting up his own home where he can make decent provision for the wife he is to acquire and the children she may bear him. A willingness to take up a vocation that does not promise this would, on the surface, be evidence that he was not the man to inject into public education the right type of masculinity; since, to be a teacher, he would have to reconcile himself to some such humiliating restriction as remaining single because of necessity or having to seek a woman willing to work for her board in order to get a husband—even of taking up a side-line such as peddling life insurance or fish.

Here we have a marked difference between the inducements that must be offered, if both Miss X and Mr. Y are to be recruited to the teaching profession. The supposition that Miss X is sincere when she insists that it hurts her professional pride to have the State offer Mr. Y a higher salary, is all rot, since her professional pride was not disturbed in the past when she stooped to use the greater financial needs of Mr. Y in order to boost her own salary. Moreover, still having in mind that the school's obligation is primarily to the child, a differentiated salary scale is justified solely in order that male teachers may enjoy the same standard of living as their female coworkers—a thing that is impossible under an equal salary scale. If Mr. Y is forced to live on a lower standard than Miss X, this sorry fact will soon become apparent to the student body. The pupils will note that Miss X dresses like a prima donna, while Mr. Y is sporting patched shoes and reseated trousers. It will not be long before Mr. Y senses their feeling of contempt and responds by developing an inferiority complex. Quickly he will be transformed into a flat-tire pedagogue.

The chief issue now stands forth as simple as a problem in elementary arithmetic: The child requires creditable male instructors; male instructors of equal worth to female pedagogues cannot be hired at the same salary; therefore, whenever the equal salary scale is put into effect it means either the men teachers will be driven out of the system or that male pedagogues of low grade will be recruited. The question here is not one of supply and demand. Typical pussyfooting college professors of education, disturbed over the failure of the schools to attract high-grade male teachers, suggest timidly that, on the score of supply and demand, perhaps a higher wage might be offered, temporarily, to males; but add, apologetically, that the solution does violence to the principles of democracy. Violence! only if the principles of democracy countenance a public school system conducted with utter disregard for the needs of the child and solely for the purpose of providing highly remunerative employment for women teachers.

Truth is that high-grade male teachers, so urgently needed in public education, cannot be attracted in any other way than by the American people boldly declaring that, in education, a larger salary must be offered the man in order to get the same quality of workers from both sexes, since inflexible economic laws command it. Without a differentiated salary scale the quality of the male will continue to drop until eventually educational systems, even of college grade, will in self-defense have to close their doors to male teachers—a state of affairs that doubtless would be highly gratifying to the women in pedagogics, regardless of the consequences to American youth.

But do not suppose that educators and school administrators surrounded by a great army of female educators, will openly advocate a differentiated scale. Thorndike[1] insists that "The choice of women over men has not been a matter of lowered standards of academic or professional training. On the contrary, there is evidence that raising the requirements quickly increases the percentage of women among those securing positions in elementary and secondary schools." Observe how cautiously the distinguished professor of Teachers College steps! No one ever presumed that the feminization of public education was accomplished through a lowering of academic standards—it got its first advantage because the State failed to pay male

[1] Op. cit.

teachers a decent salary; it made its greatest spurt when the salaries of women were made to equal those offered men. Even in Doctor Thorndike's own institution an equal salary scale would work havoc within twenty years; it would drive out all male faculty members of large ability and their places would be filled either with high-grade women or with weak-kneed men.

VI

We hear a great deal these days about the "child-centered" school from beneficiaries of a teacher-centered feminized educational system. If the public schools had been created for the benefit of those who go into teaching, then it would be truly democratic to insist upon an equal salary scale and at the same time to cease sentimental references to the child. On the other hand, if the schools actually exist for the child, it is nothing short of criminal for the American people, including school administrators, to permit a complete feminization of public education, which is bad for the child, or else to force him, wherever it is possible for him to come under the instruction of male teachers, to sacrifice his right to have as good a teacher as can be recruited to the teaching profession.

After all, the vital thing in education under democracy is not an equalization of the things offered the pedagogue, but of the things offered the child. This phase of the matter may be illuminated with a brief concrete illustration: There is a great hullabaloo about the injustice of paying Negro teachers a lower salary than is given to the whites. Asserting that under democracy there must be equality, Negro teachers, abetted by so-called liberals of the white race, demand that the State shall not discriminate between the races in the matter of teachers' salaries. But what concern to a broad-visioned democracy could be the trifling matter of having a Negro teacher get less than a white teacher of the same professional worth, provided that this is the only way to escape an enormous inequality in the educational opportunities afforded school children of the two races?

In a certain city where no race discrimination is officially allowed, the same salaries are paid to colored and white teachers. If the schools in that city are maintained for the benefit of teachers, this is justice; if they actually exist for the child, it is the rankest injustice to a part of the student body. The city's salary scale, as compared with those in other like urban systems, is not high so far as white teachers are concerned, but for Negro teachers it is away above what other cities pay. The consequence is that this city attracts from all parts of the country the very best material for Negro teachers, but its white teachers are just average. In brief, so that the Negro teacher may not have reason to believe he is discriminated against, a course is pursued which represents discrimination against all the white children of that city, since they are afforded educational opportunities inferior to those offered the Negro children—they actually sit under inferior teachers.

The real concern of democracy, when it comes to public education, should be that out of the money spent on schools each child should get an equal opportunity to learn. If a Negro woman of the same qualifications as Miss X can be engaged for $500.00 a year less, it may be that paying this lower salary appears to the Negro a penalty imposed because of the peculiar pigments in her constitution. That, however, is a matter between the Negro and her God, and something for which the white children are not responsible and should not be made to suffer. They have ground for demanding that a better grade of teacher shall not be hired for the colored children than is assigned to them, and this demand will not be met if Negro teachers are paid as much as whites. If the Negro comes back with the suggestion that, in order to make an equal salary scale possible, she be permitted to teach in white schools, the answer again, as in the case between males and females, is that a democratic school system has no business to devise such a salary schedule as, in this case, will result in making available only such white teachers as are inferior professionally to the Negroes, lest eventually public education be Africanized.

But will the public schools deal with the salary question in such manner as to do justice to the child? Will school boards courageously offer a sufficiently higher wage to male teachers so as to attract men who in all respects will be the equal of the female teachers employed, taking account of how essential it is that the child should, on the one hand, be spared from a completely feminized instructional staff, and, on the other hand, should enjoy contact with high-grade male teachers? Not by a jugful of good old rye! Back of school boards are politicians, and back of these politicians are female equalists with their cohorts daring any man in public life to disregard woman's voice when it comes to public education—"woman's divine province." With all the current gush about the child-centered school, the educational system runs no danger of being made actually to center around the interests and needs of the child, since that would mean an interference with the gradual feminization of public education, from nursery school to state-supported university —a process entirely dependent upon the equal salary scale. Rather, the child must henceforth and forever emulate little Jack Horner—he must sit in the corner pulling plums out of the public treasury and, like a nice little boy, give them to his female teacher.

CHAPTER VIII

SAMPLE SCHOOLBOOKS

A Study in Polite Graft

I

Many years ago educational publishers willfully introduced certain shady customs into their dealings with the public schools. Some of these persist; and since questionable practices on the part of those having business with the State are regarded as a very wicked thing, it might seem meet to haul the offenders into the public parks, mount them in old-fashioned stocks, and permit whoever chose to pelter them. But such a course would not be quite fair to those publishers who now are reaping tares where once they, or their predecessors, sowed perfectly good seed.

In a measure the present discussion aims to reveal the publisher in a proper light as one who is more sinned against than sinning. The reader, I hope, may be led to repress any tendency to moral indignation even over such a news item as that which lately oozed from the great State of Kentucky, where a grand jury indicted the Governor and seven other members of the State Textbook Commission, as well as twenty-five publishers, under a statute which makes it a crime for a state official who is to pass upon school books to accept "any property of value" from the publishers. The first impulse of the righteous, no doubt, was to demand blood, and especially the blood of the accused publishers. But we shall see that they are not such a bad lot. They are not villains, although maybe they once were; but now they are cast for humbler rôles of clowns.

Free textbooks, which provided the reason for the aforesaid questionable practices, are a relatively new thing in public education. Prior to the Civil War parents with children in the common schools were called on to purchase such books as their offspring required. The selection of a text then rested with either the local school trustees or individual instructors. It was not until 1873 that the principle of free textbooks won general recognition, and then to provide them became merely permissive. Eleven years later the first state made the supplying of them mandatory. To-day nineteen states prescribe that pupils must get them free, and twenty-two others authorize the local districts to buy school books out of public funds.

II

At the time when parents were still purchasing the required texts the school population was relatively small, and so only a few books were needed. The life of each book—since it was personal instead of state property—was long, and changes in the texts used were infrequent. As a consequence, the amount of trade done in schoolbooks was not great, and their publishers found no incentive for moving Heaven in order to get that business. The practice of providing textbooks free originated in the larger cities, and there it had its first substantial growth. As a natural accompaniment to this concentration of all the schoolbook business of a given city in the hands of a few officials, competition between publishers was put on a new footing. What had been a comparatively unimportant commercial line suddenly took on large proportions.

During the latter half of the Nineteenth Century, all the American cities grew rapidly, and of their expanding population a larger percentage found its way into the public schools. In a short time the situation changed, so that a pupil of the intermediate or grammar grades, instead of being called on to provide himself with a few simple texts, was supplied, at the public expense, with about as many books as he could tote to and from school.

Soon educational publishers came to look with covetous eyes on the city systems that had expanded into big book customers, and every publisher schemed how he might get a lion's share of the patronage. Where a system followed the custom of adopting a single text in a given subject, competition centered around the adoption, for the publisher who had his offering adopted got all the business on that type of book. In other systems there were what were called approved lists, and similar offerings of several publishers might win favor with the school authorities; there, after a series of texts had been approved, every publisher had to go out and fight for orders on his own book.

Of all the possible methods for getting adoptions, approvals, and orders, a few of the more aggressive and less scrupulous publishers decided that the easiest and cheapest was that of putting themselves on the good side of the officials told off to adopt, approve, or buy. With these publishers, what amounted often to downright bribery was resorted to wherever it would bring in the business. Either they went direct to school officials, bearing precious gifts, or they commissioned the local dealers in school supplies to do the dirty work for them. In any system where it was possible to introduce this graft, a publisher who preferred not to employ such means did just as well if he kept out entirely.

The readiness with which many schoolmen coöperated with the more affable and liberal publishers is quickly explained. In those days a large majority of the men holding administrative school positions were primarily politicians. They got their appointments through politics, and their positions, like most other political jobs, paid less than any really competent man deserved. An incumbent might elect to lead a virtuous life and be annoyed forever by the howls of the wolf outside his door, or he might follow the ways that invited for supplementing his meagre income. No one sensed the situation better than the publishers, and more than a few of them set up as good Samaritans willing to go to the succor of such school officials. The consequence was that many a schoolman fell—into more comfortable circumstances.

As the volume of book business in any given system expanded, competition for it among publishers grew keener, so that in certain communities the possible rake-off took on sufficient proportions to become alluring even to the higher sort of professional politicians. It was then that boards of education, in many instances, relieved the superintendent of responsibility for selecting and buying textbooks and supplies, and took the burden on their own shoulders. A school commissioner who could see nothing iniquitous in demanding a substantial fee from a candidate for a teaching position before nominating him, naturally saw no harm, when he came to deal with publishers, in permitting them to touch with gold the unsalaried position he had accepted on a lay board—because of a dynamic sense of civic duty.

The natural sequence was that publishers in due course sought to take a hand in the politics of every community where they had succeeded in working their game. In order that a publisher might secure the cream of the book orders from a given system, he wanted his say about who should be named as school commissioners and superintendent, and the logical course was to help finance the election of public officials, governors, mayors, legislators, and city councilmen—the men who were to appoint school authorities and pass on school expenditures.

III

Thus in those good old days, a lot of lamentable work went on in connection with the schoolbook business. Almost as colorful as the tales of horse thieves from an earlier period are some of the stories that could be related. One incident will be set forth here to indicate the wealth of the material which will be lost to posterity forever when the last of the old schoolbook agents is gathered unto the bosom of Abraham. At the time of this incident, the contest for the control of corrupted systems had reached such a point that the instant a year's orders had been placed, half a dozen disappointed publishers would pull their hair and yell: "Crook!" "Thief!" Incidentally, it was not always the same publisher who won such denunciation.

At that time only a few of the larger publishers maintained branches in different sections of the country. Each such branch had its own clerical and sales forces, and handled the business originating in the territory assigned to it. One day, on the occasion of a visit by the executives of, say, the Paragon Publishing House to one of its branches, the auditor discovered a shortage in the accounts. When the local cashier was put on the mat, he admitted having borrowed from the till; but always with the intention of paying back just so soon as convenient. He resented having his superiors refer to him as an embezzler. The fact that he wrote an *I. O. U.* each time he took a wad of greenbacks from the drawer, proved that he was not crooked. But the officials wanted only honest men in their clerical departments and promptly dismissed him. Moreover, he was warned that unless he made the shortage good within twenty-four hours he would be turned over to the police.

The poor fellow went forth to raise a sum of slightly more than seven hundred dollars; but his friends were honest and poor, and could not help him. At the end of the allotted time, he returned and explained to his principals that his mission had failed. Their faces hardened. In that case, his destination was jail; they would call the police immediately. The cashier neither lost his schoolboy complexion nor begged for mercy, but, with an audacity which his employers had to admire, told them something.

Their attitude toward him, he said, was unfair; their accusations were unwarranted, for at heart he was as honest as the day was long, and a faithful employee to boot. Unfortunately, circumstances did not always do him justice, but over such circumstances he had no control. For instance, the very night before, after his dismissal and while he was gathering up his few belongings—calico sleeves, leather apron, and eye-shade—certain important papers belonging to the firm somehow got mixed up with his personal property. He discovered them on his arrival home. As he enumerated a few of the items, consternation spread over the group of men facing him. His recital was interrupted so that an official might go to the office and explore the private files. When he returned, a gloomy nod of his head indicated that the fellow was telling the truth. Certain very important documents were not in their accustomed places.

Had the cashier brought them back? No; his first impulse had been to do so, but he realized that any explanation he might offer as to how these papers got into his possession would surely be rejected by men who were determined to see him as a common thief. Well, what did he propose doing with them? Perhaps, after he had been sent to jail, his wife would go out and peddle them, so as to raise money to provide the necessities of life for herself and her children. Poor woman! she'd need it badly then.

There was a whispered conference while the dismissed cashier looked out the window and hummed a tune. Then one of the officials wondered if it would not be more sensible for the cashier himself to sell the documents, and escape going to jail. He had, it appeared, thought of that. What price did he ask? Fifteen thousand dollars. The officials laughed, and the cashier asked, blandly, whether they regarded the figure as too low. They said they would pay five thousand, ask no questions, and forget the shortage. No! Then, eight. No! Well, ten—but that was the limit. The cashier, however, insisted that the papers were worth every cent of fifteen thousand dollars—if not to the Paragon Publishing House, then to one of its competitors. All right; if he was so mercenary as to exact an exorbitant price, they would submit to the extortion rather than prolong the conference. He was to take the papers then to a certain lawyer next morning who, on receiving them and getting the cashier's signature to a legal acknowledgment, would pay him the ransom money.

The lawyer mentioned was a notorius shyster, but, despite this, the following morning the dismissed employee took his way to his office, bundle under arm. A group of toughs, ostensibly clients waiting to see the lawyer, crowded the corridor just outside the door. As the cashier attempted to gain entrance, one of the group jostled him roughly and then began to curse him. A score of men closed in on him, threatening to beat him up unless he apologized. Meekly he apologized, and they moved off. But during the altercation,

SAMPLE SCHOOLBOOKS 179

the package had been taken from beneath his arm. And then, instead of making his intended call on the lawyer, he went back to the office of the Paragon Publishing House and reported the affair.

"That's too bad," the general manager told him, "but, of course, we can't give you fifteen thousand dollars unless you recover and deliver to us the stolen papers." The cashier smiled slyly. He had not said the papers had been taken from him, but that a bundle he carried under his arm had been stolen. Meditating on the matter the previous evening, he had wondered if it would be discreet to trust the negotiations to the attorney the firm named; therefore, instead of carrying the papers with him that morning, he had made up a dummy of blanks. The dummy had been stolen. "Moreover, I have decided not to sell the papers—to you!"

With that he walked out of the office. No one attempted to obstruct his way; the shortage was never mentioned again; the dismissed cashier immediately afterwards went into business on his own account, and appeared to have ample capital. Tradition is that these papers are still a treasured possession of another educational publisher. The change in their ownership had a most salutary influence on the attitude of publishers toward one another. Thereafter, no matter how violently politicians, schoolmen, and the lay public might denounce them for their shady methods, they always spoke of one another as gentlemen. Graft in the schoolbook business had been put on a plane of dignity.

IV

Times have changed. Only occasionally now does a publisher or his agent attempt to buy schoolbook orders. This, however, is not to be interpreted as evidence that money no longer passes from a publisher, or his representative, to a schoolman. Now and then it does.

Not so long ago a school official, discussing graft in the book business, made the point that if a schoolman today gets a rake-off, the thing can hardly be regarded as harmful in the same sense that it formerly was. In the earlier days, he explained, many textbooks were poor, and, where a mediocre text won out because its publisher offered the biggest bonus, the dear little school children suffered. But now nearly all schoolbooks have some merit, and so, even though a discreet gift may be the factor which gives one offering the preference over others, the children still get a fairly decent book. Perhaps this schoolman was interested only in the theory of the thing and, also perhaps, he was trying on others a line of logic which he had panned off successfully on his own conscience.

But there are reasons outside the realm of morality which explain why educational publishers no longer provide slush funds in such wise as was once their wont. Conditions are radically different. Thirty and forty years ago the cost of the product was inconsequential. If the manufactured book cost a publisher more than one sixth its selling price, he felt there was something wrong. Again, legitimate selling costs were not so high then. When salesmen talked *turkey* instead of books, they got through more quickly and landed the orders. Now the representative of an educational publisher must be a high-grade man who knows intimately not only the works offered by his firm, but those of other publishers as well—knows them in the same practical way as if he had used them in class.

Finally, most contemporary school officials are well paid and, even if one were disposed to increase his income, he would hardly hazard his position and professional standing for a small piece of money. Even in Kentucky, where eight members of the Textbook Commission and twenty-five publishers were indicted, it is doubtful if money actually passed, or was offered, in a single instance. What, then, was all the hullabaloo about?

Books—free books—endless bundles of books passing from publishers to school officials without cost to the recipient. This giving of books free appears an altogether harmless thing in the light of a statement issued by the Kentucky Textbook Commission after certain of its members had been indicted:

There is no pretense . . . that the members of the commission, or any of them, received anything save the usual sample books—one of a kind, always provided and sent members of the Textbook Commission of Kentucky and other States under like circumstances so that the books may be examined and the commission determine which books shall be adopted.

This sounds fair enough; but the explanation conceals a practice which was born in sin and has steadfastly refused to be cleansed of the iniquity of its origin. When the publishers in the earlier years were doling out gold to those school officials who could be reached in that way, they were not always able actually to land the business through corrupted officials. Where a system had an approved list which contained several texts suitable for the same grade in a subject, the orders any one publisher got on his offerings depended upon the demand made by various schools for that book. Therefore, even if graft had played a part in putting his book on the approved list, there remained the problem of getting orders for it.

This publisher could scarcely go and, with cash money, "insult" every teacher who might be in a position to select his text over those of his competitors. He could have his representative call on the teachers and, in the case of men, set up the drinks; in the case of women, buy candy; but that would have been a clumpsy procedure. Therefore, to humor a teacher by making him feel he was getting something for nothing, and thus create a kindly attitude toward the publisher who gave this something, the scheme was devised of giving away books. The instant it was put into operation, teachers took to it with avidity, and were soon asking for books—books—books, and getting them. It did not take the publishers long to realize that they had started a costly practice, especially as many of the volumes sent out on request could not possibly be considered by the recipient for classroom use, and no business could result.

V

Then a Little Napoleon of the craft proposed a remedy. If all publishers would simultaneously stop the practice—that very year—the school people would have to accept the change in good grace, and the publishers would patch up a very serious leakage in their business. So there was an implied agreement between the larger publishers that thereafter no books would be sent out unsolicited, while requests for examination copies would be honored only in cases where there was a possibility of the work being adopted for classes.

But just when the teachers were making up their minds—and requisitions—on books to be ordered the next term, the house with which the Little Napoleon was associated simply flooded the educational field with unsolicited free books. It was a clever trick, pulled after months of secret preparation, and the firm that year harvested a bumper crop of orders. But since that day every educational publisher becomes leery the moment somebody suggests a discontinuance of the practice of sending books to school people for nothing. Today the tradition is that not only a schoolman who is to pass on texts for general use, but any teacher who asks an educational publisher for "examination" copies, has a right to expect that the request will be honored promptly and cheerfully. The publishers realize that there is an unsavory odor to the thing, yet they continue to submit.

Some time ago a leading educational publisher received a request for an elementary textbook which, so the applicant said, was to be examined to determine if he could use it in his classes. It happened in this case that the book in question had exclusive adoption in the town from which the request came, while the publisher's records did not list the correspondent as either an official or teacher in the school system. But the publisher—a big corporation—feared to take the chance of offending a teacher by refusing the request or asking for information as to the correspondent's status. The book was dispatched, and the representative who solicited business in that town was instructed to look up the writer on his next visit. Several weeks later he discovered that the letter had been written by a schoolboy of thirteen who had lost the copy of this particular text that had been provided by the school. He was told he must replace it, and, either because he was just an ordinary thief or else had the makings of a pedagogue, he decided that the simplest and cheapest course to pursue was to ask for an "examination" copy from the publisher.

This form of benign graft—originated by publishers long years ago, and now come home to afflict them—has become so firmly imbedded in the thinking of American pedagogues that in numerous instances librarians and other officials of educational institutions have printed mailing cards instructing publishers to send them such books as they may list "provided there is no charge." The president of a large state institution once confessed that its library got most of its accessions by such means. Since publishers apparently lacked the courage to refuse his demands for books without cost, this official saw no need to go to the legislature and ask for such appropriations as would remove the need for his grafting. In a training school for teachers a visitor found the pupils of the model school using a cheap and nearly obsolete reader. He asked why such a wretched classroom tool was being used in an institution engaged in training teachers, and was informed that the publisher of the particular text was the only one willing to *give* a sufficient number of books to supply the entire class.

The Superintendent of Public Instruction in a prosperous western state is forever sending letters to publishers suggesting that if this or that book is sent him free, he will be glad to recommend it to the teachers in his state. If publishers had courage, they would see the humor in such a proposal; they would promptly ask this official how much weight a recommendation by a grafting superintendent could be expected to have with his subordinates. But instead they send books and see only tragedy in the situation. Under the shadow of the wing of this noble official has sprung up a nice little female pedagogue who writes polite notes asking publishers please to send her a "courtesy" copy of any book which strikes her gentle feminine fancy.

The average teacher finds it easy to persuade himself that he not only should get a free "desk copy" of any book he may possibly find suitable for use by his students, but also "examination" copies of works he may think to read for either pleasure or professional growth. How can he tell whether a new book may or may not be useful to him, except he read it? Why should he pay for a book to read when the publisher stands a chance, no matter how slight, of getting orders for additional copies, should he find the volume appealing? Moreover, it is the publisher's business to make his profits on books going to students, not on those to pedagogues.

So firmly is the average American educator convinced that publishers should give him books without cost, that he does not hesitate to tell anyone who dares to refuse his demands that he will use no more texts bearing the imprint of that house and will urge his associates to join in the boycott.

VI

An insignificant pedagogue is appointed to teach, say, modern history in a small college. Immediately he writes to various educational publishers, on the institution's stationery, explaining that he is seeking a good basic text for his course; also supplementary readings in history, civics, sociology, economics, and whatnot. He may send out ten, twenty, or thirty such letters, and even indicate at length the specific titles on this or that publisher's list which he thinks may prove suitable. He may receive, in response to these letters, fifty, a hundred, or a hundred fifty books—in short, a sufficiently comprehensive library in his field to reveal to him, if ever he takes the time to read half the volumes, the meagreness of the scholarship on which he gained his appointment. Examining the "samples" casually, he selects one, not because of its merit perhaps, but because the price is low and it is "easy to teach." In due course, the college sends in an order for five copies—that number representing the size of the young instructor's class. Obviously, the transaction has not been profitable to the publisher whose book is adopted, and certainly not to the other firms which responded to the request.

But the thing does not stop here. The youthful pedagogue has discovered how easy it is to get books for the asking, and concludes that any additional works he may want during the balance of his college career will doubtless come to him without cost through writing letters occasionally. Eventually, he does not bother to infer that the book asked for is to be examined with a view to use in his own class; he may wish to examine it simply with thought of recommending it to others. When this instructor marries and goes to housekeeping, he furnishes his home with books from cellar to dome, and at no expense.

The grafting goes even further. When the pedagogue finds that he can accumulate a lot of books free, and sees enormous stacks of them about him for which he cannot afford shelf space, Satan comes along and says: Why not sell them? He thanks Satan for the suggestion and goes in quest of a customer. He finds a number of establishments specially organized for buying "examination" copies of educational books from people of his kind. He opens negotiations with such a concern, and when the first check comes in is stirred to assemble another batch of books for shipment. Eventually, his one problem is to get books enough to maintain profitable relations with this secondhand book company.

The concerns which thus buy books from schoolmen are most efficient. They are forever appealing to the teacher for an opportunity to bid on such sample copies as he receives. On the other hand, they watch closely the demand for books from educational institutions. Recently, a publishing house got out a new high-school text just about the time books were being ordered for a school term. This book was approved immediately by one city system, which invited bids on four hundred copies. The publisher quoted his usual price on that quantity, but when the bids were opened, he was amazed to find that the order went to a jobber who, to complete it, had to purchase thirty odd copies from the publisher. The remainder of the four hundred copies had been procured at low prices from those who, either on request or without solicitation, had received examination copies!

Perhaps this discussion has illuminated for the reader the Kentucky incident. When the exposé occurred in the Blue Grass, one of the indicted members of the Textbook Commission pooh-poohed the whole affair as "a matter of politics." Said he:

I received no money from publishers. I sold to a second-hand book concern at Chicago for $325 a quantity of books submitted to me by book publishers. I had a number of books—arithmetics, spellers, and grammars—for which I had no use. Some books for high-school work I kept.[1]

The amusing thing is that the specimen books sent to this pedagogue in his official capacity, and disposed

[1] Associated Press despatch from Lexington, Ky., September 19, 1929.

of as personal property, apparently were volumes he did not even examine. His duty was to pass on *secondary* school books, but he got enough samples of *elementary* texts to net him $325. The reader may speculate as to the quantity of spellers, arithmetics, and grammars—the least costly of elementary texts—that must have reached him for him to realize $325; also how much business these perfectly new "second-hand" books took from the *educational* publishers, as their tribute to Caesar.

As the Textbook Commission, in its comment on the indictments, intimates, the situation is not peculiar to Kentucky. A few months before the State of North Carolina gave a similar performance. An approved list for the entire State, covering a period of five years, was prepared; and from this list the various educational units were to make their choice of several works on the same subject. Not only did the publishers, in their scramble for business, load the State with all the representatives they could take from other districts, but they poured in carloads of samples. What became of these books? A considerable portion was promptly converted into cash, and this cash went into the private pockets of schoolmen.

Some educators were frank in their declaration that they proposed selling the samples to pay them for the bother of opening and looking at them. They ignored the fact that they were also paid by the State or their respective school systems for this performance. A local bookseller approached some of the publishers with an offer to buy up all of their samples that he could find afloat in the State, provided they would give him 75 per cent of the list price for them. They rejected the proposition. They did not dare send out books acquired in this way as new copies; more important, they would have gone bankrupt if they had paid 75 per cent of the list price, for, taking account of their discounts to schools, it was much more than they actually charged.

Here, as in the good old days, the publisher who got the business made his contribution in the equivalent of perfectly good money; but the publishers who got no orders also perforce helped to swell the graft fund. Here is the rub, since the unsuccessful competitors find themselves filling the humiliating rôles of suckers.

VII

Of course, there may be a silver lining to the cloud. Some day the situation may clear up, not through the efforts of publishers, since they lack the courage to attempt to correct the graft for fear that they may lose a customer here and there, but through an awakening sense of decency on the part of schoolmen. Attempting to get a little extra money through begging sample books and then selling them at a ridiculously low price is just a little less dignified than accepting a cash rake-off such as was offered in earlier years.

Even now a story goes the rounds of one man in education who thinks it beneath him to accept free books from publishers who are soliciting his patronage on their offerings. When a sample book reaches him, he is courteous enough to look at it. If the book interests him, he insists on paying for it; if it does not, he returns it, charges collect. Although a snicker is occasionally heard when schoolmen and book agents discuss this exceptional educator, he may be the forerunner of the American educator of the future. There is no law against supposing that his tribe may increase. Perhaps in the next generation, there may be three such educators. Or even four.

INDEX

ADAMS, JOHN SMITH, sits for portrait of a typical college president....... 17

Administrative and supervisory departments grow corpulent on juicy budgets 68

Adult education, a domain on which the sun never sets 78

Alumni may be a nuisance, as in the case of the expert, 5. Also of one Louie Swartzheimer ... 22

American Legion produces a strenuous reformer...142

Attendance records faked to win promotion and pay 134

AYRES, LEONARD P., establishes quantitativeness as an educational ideal.... 60

Baker shop becomes a school laboratory 98

BALLOU, SUPERINTENDENT FRANK W., reveals a backbone 143

Baltimore SUN defends "extravagances and vagaries" 6

Beauty queen contest on a dignified basis 110

BENNETT, PROFESSOR G. VERNON, discovers a money-spending sideline 77

BRIGGS, THOMAS H., recommends mixed faculties..157

BUMP, PROFESSOR HORATIO, essays the rôle of a great educationist 12

Bureau of Education becomes an "Office" to soften idea of bureaucracy 38

Business has no business to prescribe curricula 114

BUTLER, PRESIDENT NICHOLAS MURRAY, explains education for democracy 125

Butter-and-egg man is won to educational extravagance 64

Cabinet job for pedagogues justified by Honorable Arthur Capper 35

INDEX

Cabinet member revealed in his edifying daily life. 47

Cabinet membership proposed to give educational leadership dignity...... 32

CAPPER, HONORABLE ARTHUR, "goes on the air". 35

Cafeteria patronage properly taught............ 99

Caterpillar crawls into the curriculum 97

Cheese boxes as educational test material.......... 96

Chewing gum attracts the creative budget makers. 73

Child-centered school with the child left out....... 166

Chipmunk enters the sixth grade 107

Citizenship training by shackled teachers 128, easy when stupid 122, under despotic administrators 132

Classroom instruction and size of class........... 138

Clean-speech campaigns should be emotional.... 112

Collegiate training for undertakers and railway-station agents 78

Commission on the Emergency in Education..... 30

Communists get a "wallop" from Major General Fries 142

Cost accepted as the gauge for educational progress 60, not a criterion for judging beauty 4

CRABTREE, JAMES WILLIAM, qualifies as a magician.. 41

Creative administration fattens the budget 63, has a big job ahead.......... 75

Creative budget-making is a real man's task....... 74

Dancing according to approved standards....... 113

DAVIS, MARY DABNEY, shows how a Federal employee should walk..... 38

Department of Superintendence stages undignified scramble for honor positions .... 49 See also National Education Association.

DEWEY, JOHN, leaves an idea loose for Professor Bump 12

Education as the bulwark for democracy 121, may be unfriendly to democracy 121

INDEX

Education Bill of the Smith-Towner label.... 30

Educational leadership ineffectual at present 19, 24, 28

Eighteenth Amendment mentioned without prejudice 123

English instruction staged as a joke.............. 95

Equal salaries and the Negro teacher 167

Equal salaries prevent the hiring of efficient men teachers 161, produce unequal quality in teaching force 164, 167, *versus* unequal requirements of teachers 162, win approval of American Democracy 150

Equality of educational opportunity and school building costs 6, for white and Negro pupils 168, *versus* equal salaries. 166

Ethics allowed to nourish quackery 25, 28

Ethics for teachers used as a muzzle............. 136

Experiments substituted for proved procedures...... 7

Experts take orders from prejudiced laymen..... 5

Factory conception of a teachers' college 21

Fads and idle women.... 28

Fads: study of a moist one and how it was put over 13

Family's private affairs as classroom material 105

FARRELL, MAJOR JOHN A., assumes a heroic pose..147

Federal Department of Education scheme being deserted by earlier vociferous advocates ... 8

FLINT, JOHN KNOX, a trustee who dislikes evolutionists 21

FLURY, HENRY, dares to define socialism 141

FORD, HENRY, gets a bouquet from a Major General 142

Frankfurter, the modest "hot dog," gets educational 23

Free textbooks as housefurnishings 188, in the United States 171, become a medium of graft. 181

FRIES, MAJOR GENERAL AMOS A., gets vigorous. 141

GOLDBACK, MARCUS, a trustee who likes quacks... 21

INDEX

Goose-step loyalty in various forms 135, 137, 139, 147

HILL, PROFESSOR PATTY SMITH, pictures a glorious age for the baby school 82
Hoover's Commission on Law Observance and Enforcement gets broken-reed support 41

ICHABOD comes to life as a portfolio aspirant 56
Intercity rivalry as a means for boosting school costs 63

JOHNSON, MARIETTE, talks about when love comes to school 117
JONES, SAM, a type of student who does not profit by Progressive education 89
Junior colleges have unlimited field for money-spending 77

Kentucky State Textbook Commission is surveyed by a grand jury 170, but tells all about sample books 181

Leadership based on political appointment not adequate for present needs 46, 57, cheap methods of determining in outstanding educational groups. 48
Leisure, education for, may produce a hobo........ 77
Liberal Club at West Chester displays the "Spirit of '76" 147
Libraries built on schoolbook graft 185
Lindbergh, Colonel Charles A., receives some gush.. 51
Little Jack Horner in a new rôle 169
Los Angeles Course of Study quoted 90
Loyalty as an excuse for professional inaction ... 26

Male teachers desirable in educational system 157, now in service inferior to females 159, becoming extinct on account of equal salary scales..... 164
Mary's Little Lamb accorded sympathy for its treatment by an old-style schoolmaster 14

North Carolina looks at some textbooks 190

INDEX

Nursery schools cry for more money 82
NATION, MRS. CARRIE, and her hatchet reappear momentarily 153
National Education Association meeting loaded to elect a female 48, avoids sex discrimination 50, sponsors a Federal department of education 39, wears blinders when studying liquor question 40 See also Department of Superintendence.
Negro teachers and equal salaries 167
Newspapers are gluttons for bizarre school news. 16
Night schools allow Progressive education to waste the day......... 89
Nineteenth Amendment appears to justify equal salaries 154

Office of Education casts shadows of coming events 39

Paper drives to buy victrolas on the instalment plan 108

Paragon Publishing House's cashier gets into a tight corner 176, but wiggles out 179
Patriotic societies interfere with teachers' freedom. 129
Pedagogues and the temptation to get books free 187, dare not be real democrats 127, defend quacks to protect their own hides 2
Pedagogy adopts the methods of the go-getter..... 64
Petology — a typical fad that grew like a weed.. 14
Pets not sufficiently utilized by earlier educators.... 15
Pierce University affords fertile soil for foolish fads 17
Politics in conferring educational honors 49
Preschool child passes judgment on a Progressive school plant 85, education discussed enthusiastically by Professor Patty Smith Hill 82
Progressive education competes with Emily Post as an authority on etiquette 102, measures its attainments in other things

than common school subjects 115, opens the school doors to a chipmunk 107, stages a great paper drive 109, takes the fragrance out of perfumery 103, teaches proper toilet practices 98, 105, also how to convert discarded underwear into cats and dolls 99, also intricacies of doll stuffing . 106

Progressive school systems follow l a t e s t fashion news 67

Promotion won subserviently 132

Public school administration undemocratic 124

Public schools maintained for benefit of teachers or pupils? 155

Public's influence on weakkneed pedagogues 19

Publishers introduce shady practices into schoolbook business 170

Pupils' rights ignored under equal salary scales . . 155

PYRTLE, E. RUTH, makes a daring stab at Lady Nicotine 50, places a wreath on the head of Colonel Lindbergh 51

Quackery in education illustrated by a sketch of Professor Horatio Bump 12, revealed by the National Education Association's encounter with John Barleycorn 42

Quacks given right of way by substantial educators 17

Quantitativeness made the ideal of education 60

REED, HONORABLE DANIEL A., regards school buildings as of more importance than hen houses . . 33

Research appears in person, but with false whiskers 39

Research of creditable character now being carried on 43, but those who might profit by it are cold 44, played up in later editions of the Educational Bill 32, under Federal control necessarily handicapped 37

Retardation explained 131, a clever scheme for its elimination 132

Revolt of youth a possible consequence of over-

INDEX

feminized public education 157
Ringmasters of education crack the whip 33
Safety First by running and leaping 106
Saint Louis Curriculm Bulletins tell wonders of Progressive education .. 90
Salaries considered in the light of sex and color of the pedagogue 153, that disregard sex may be unfair to pupils 166
Sample school books converted into cash 189
Satan pays a fleeting visit to the pedagogue 188
School boards should be elected, says Shankland. 54
Schoolbook graft in the good old days 175, produces a second Napoleon 183; see also Kentucky School Book Commission, North Carolina, Paragon Publishing House; publishers take a hand in politics 174
School buildings judged by size and cost 5, 65
School costs and incomes of individuals 73, discussed by National Education Association "Experts" 71, may not be debated calmly 69, must be justified 70, phenomenal increase of 62
Seatwork for mother's headgear 94
Secretaryship of Education advocated as essential to needed research 44, also to give leadership dignity 46, also to unify educational activities of United States Government 55, why a real educational leader could not accept the job 47, why he would not be offered the job 48
SHANKLAND, SHERWOOD D., says a few things 54
Slogan making should be encouraged 112
SMALL, PROFESSOR LAWRENCE, wrestles weakly with quackery 24
SMITH, ANDREW THOMAS, predicted that somebody would get knocked on the head 146
Smith-Hughes Vocational Act aids the cripples of Progressive education .. 89

INDEX

Smith-Towner Educational Bill 30
SNEDDEN, DAVID, discusses the need for male teachers 157
Social polish under Progressive education 93
Socialism discussed by the ignorant 141
State colleges help fatten the budget 76
STRAYER, GEORGE D., talks about school costs...... 58
Superintendent, autocratic powers of 131, concerned about holding on 28, 129, may be a despot. 130
SWARTZHEIMER, LOUIE, the type of alumnus who wants to run things.... 22

Teacher now a word of feminine gender 152
Teachers cowardly under autocratic administration 132, denied freedom to express personal views 127, 135, muzzled by their jobs 148, not to interfere with child's self-education 91, freedom restricted under present-day education 125, restriction denied 3

Tenure of office important to a superintendent....130
THORNDIKE, EDWARD L., sees advantage in mixed faculties 157, touches cautiously the question of equal salaries........165
Three R's meet the Three P's 16
Toy making as a school activity 99
Trustees of a college know not how to run the institution 18
Trustees—see Marcus Goldbach, John Knox Flint, Louis Swartzheimer.

Voting as a criterion of good citizenship 123

WATSON, PROFESSOR JOHN B., has a scheme for turning out Beethovens instead of shoemakers.. 81
West Chester Normal School has a rumpus...146
Window gazing as an educational project 92, 117
WINSLOW, SUPERINTENDENT ISAAC O., makes a lunge at the author.... 3